Pin-Ups vs Zombies Adult Coloring Book

Mark Anthony Brewer

Copyright© 2016 by Mark Anthony Brewer/Brewtaniusink

All right reserved. No part of tis publication may be produced, distributed, or transmitted in any form or by any means, including photocopying, recording, or other electronic or mechanical methods, without the prior written permission of the publisher, except in the case of brief quotations embodied in critical reviews and certain other non-commercial uses permitted by copyright law. For permission requests, write to the publisher address "Attention: Permission Coordinator" at the address below.

Brewtanius Ink
1135 W. Sheridan Ave
Chicago IL, 60660
www.brewtaniusink.com

Ordering Information:
Quantity Sales Special discounts are available on quantity purchases by corporations associations, and others for details. Contact publisher at the address above. Orders by U.S. trade bookstores and wholesalers. Please contact Brewtanius Ink: Tel: (847) 794-8036; www.brewtaniusink@gmail.com or visit www.brewtaniusink.com

Printed in the United States of America

Coloring Ideas

- Color Pencils or Crayons: These will work on the pages this book without worry of bleed through. If you use these you can keep all the designs in the book when you are coloring them.
- Markers: If you prefer to use makers you will need to either put a couple of sheets of paper under the sheet you with to color so that it won't bleed through to the next page, or you can cut the page out and color it without worrying about it bleeding on another sheet in the book.

Uses for Finished Sheets

You can use the finished sheets to make all kinds of other art. Here are just a few ideas!

- Gift tags: Use a finished sheet to cut out page shapes for unique gift tags.
- Bookmarks: cut the finished sheet in half then cut each half into four equal pieces and laminate them for cute handmade bookmarks!
- Gift Wrap: do you have a small gift that you would like to have a unique wrapping paper for? Then use one of your completed pages to wrap the gift and add some ribbons to make a cute bow.

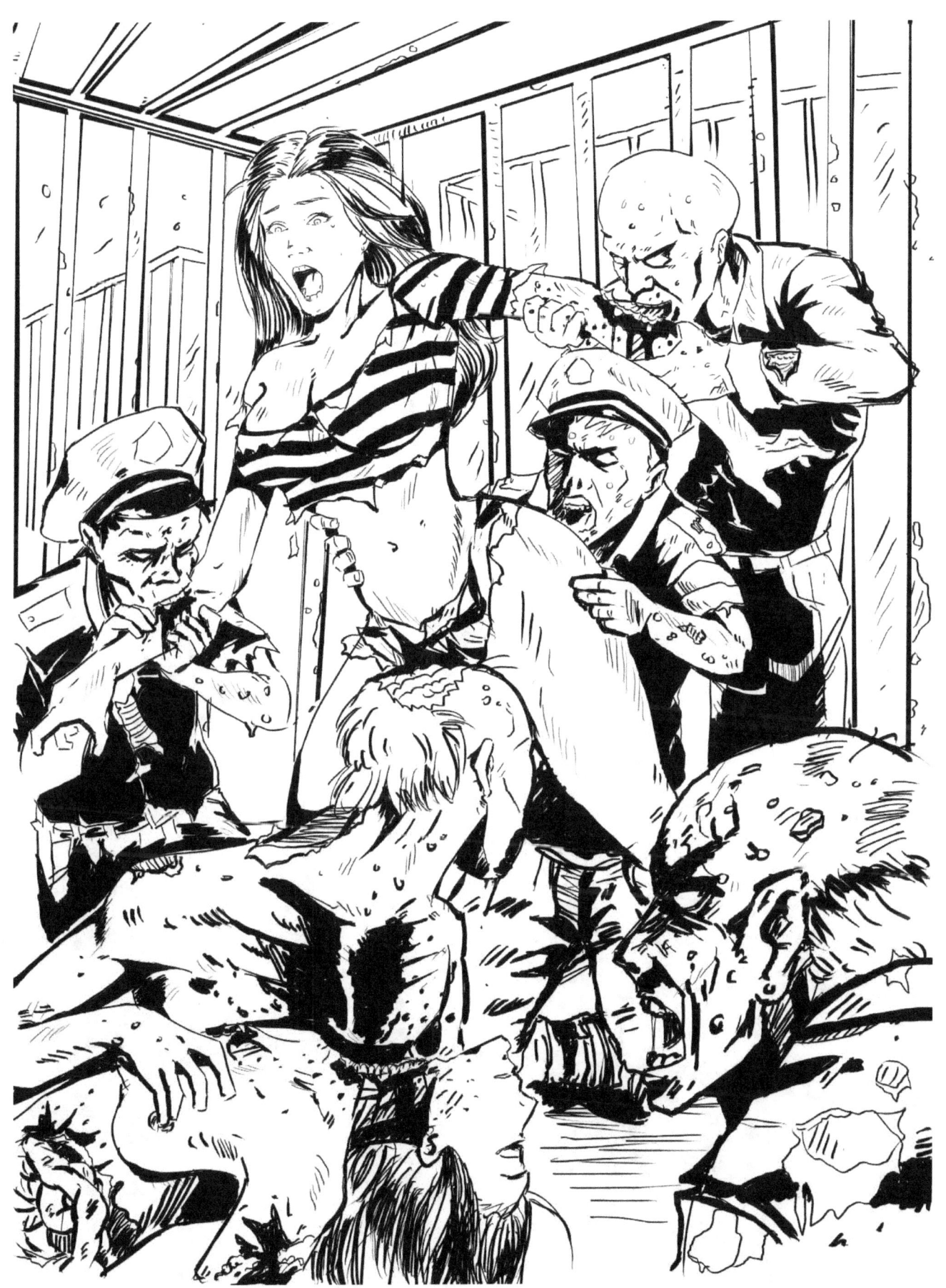

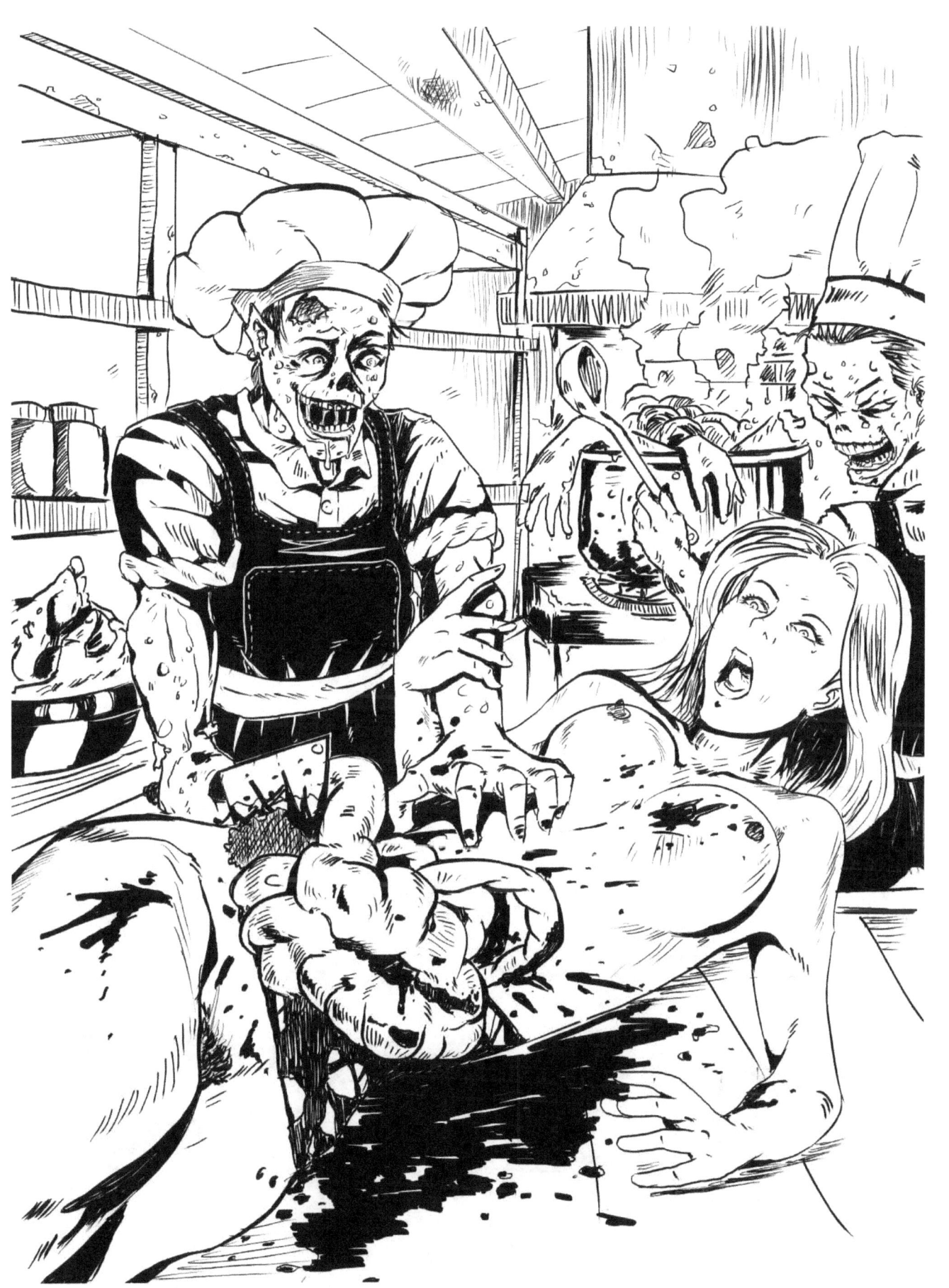

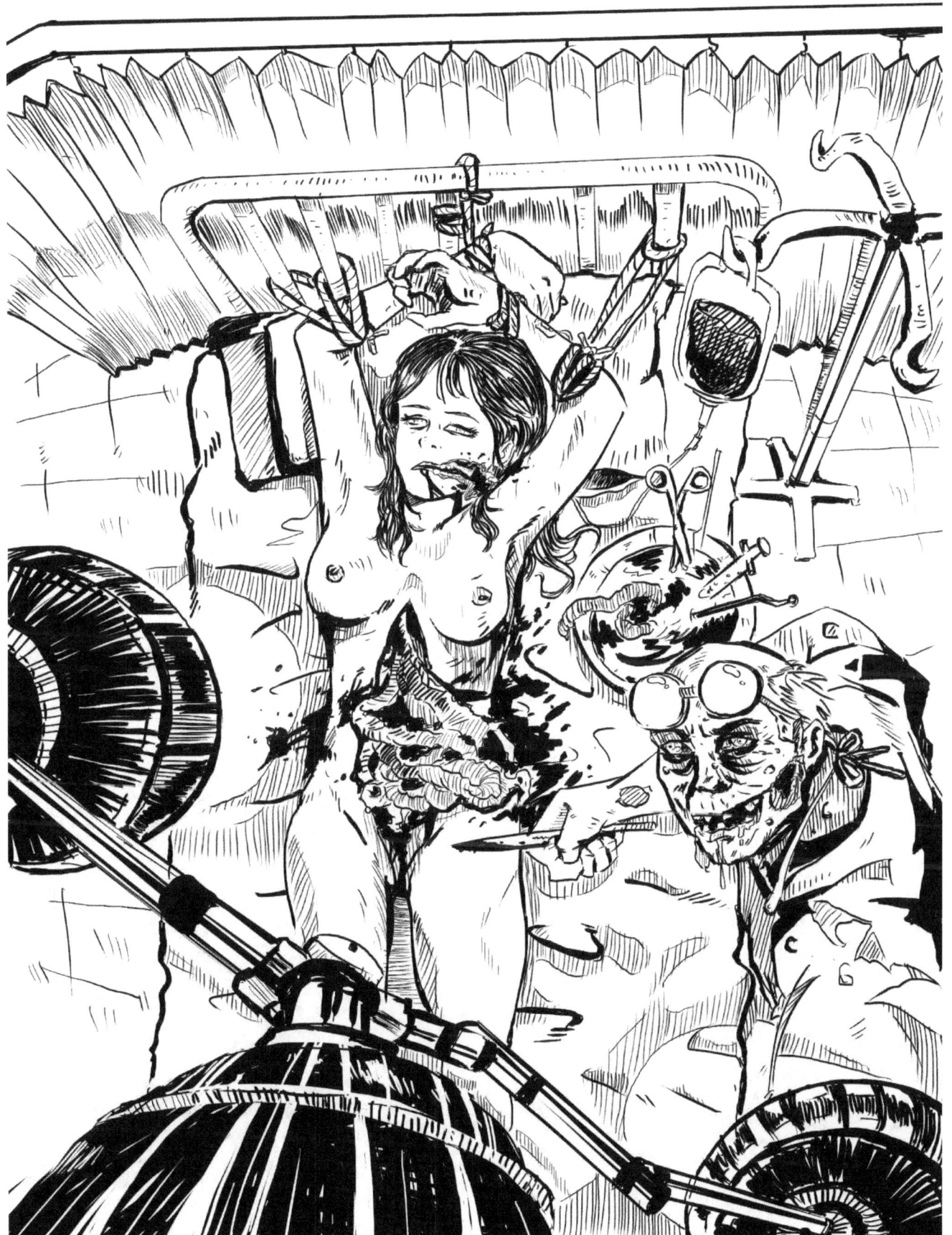

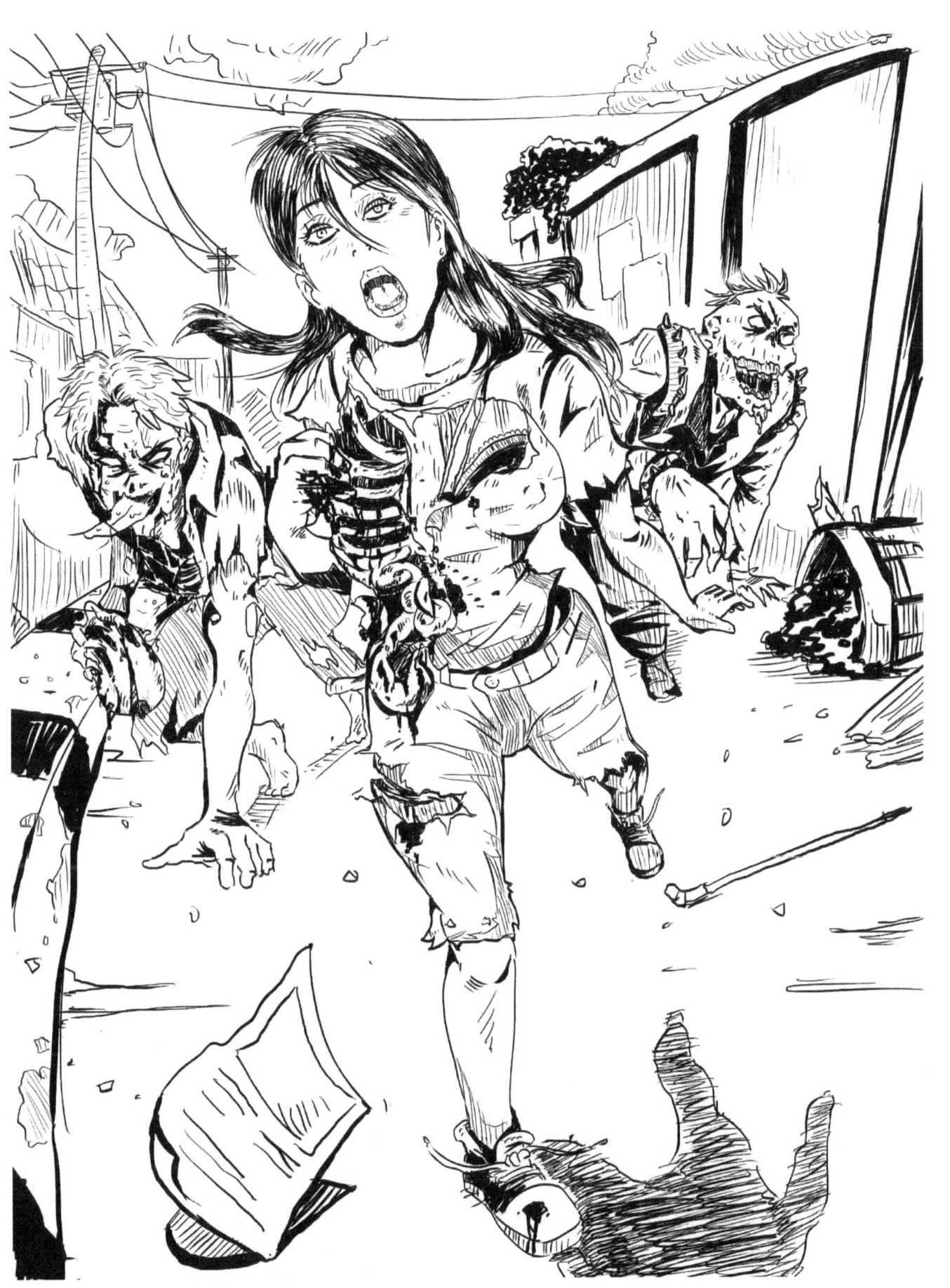

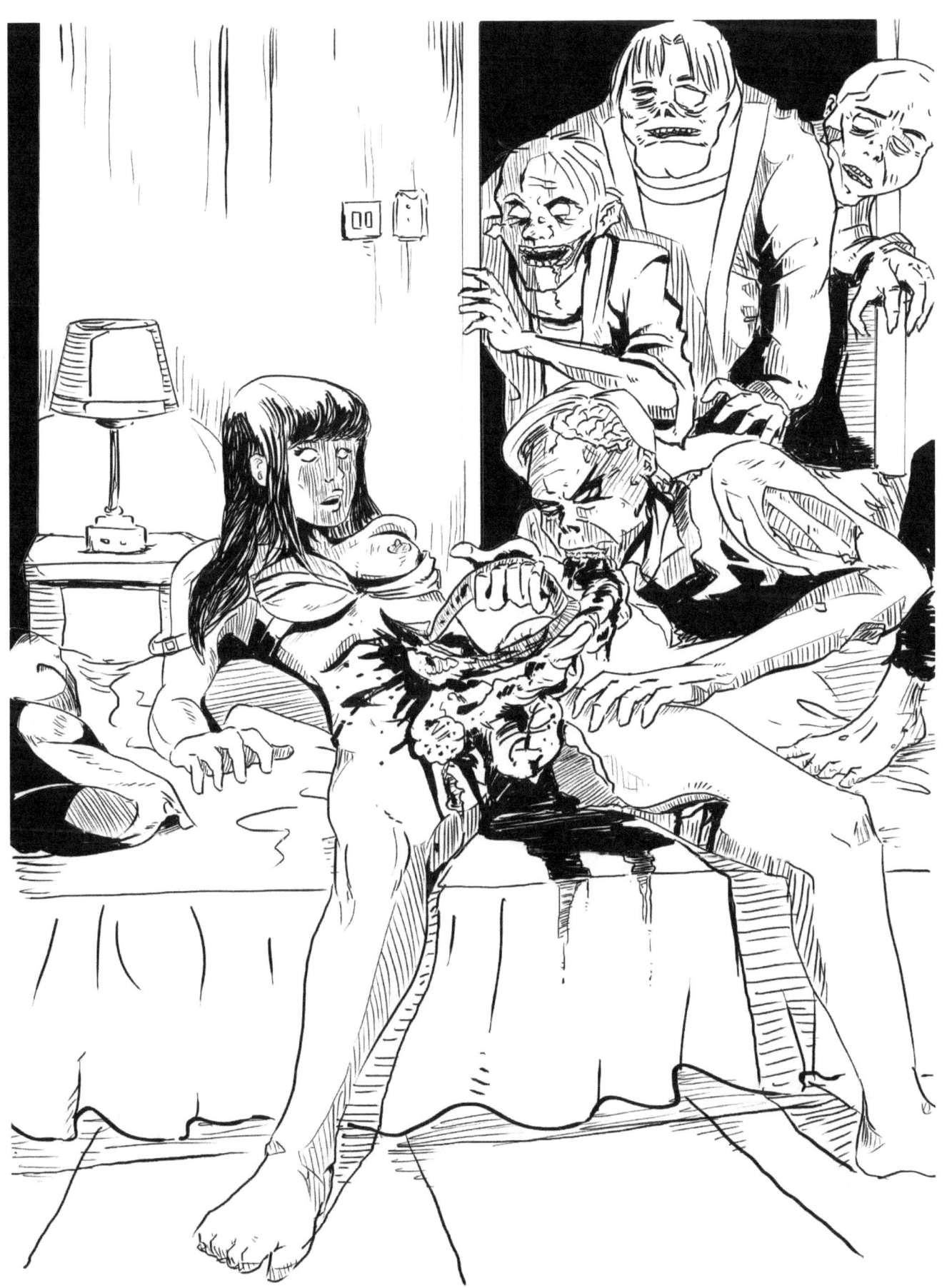

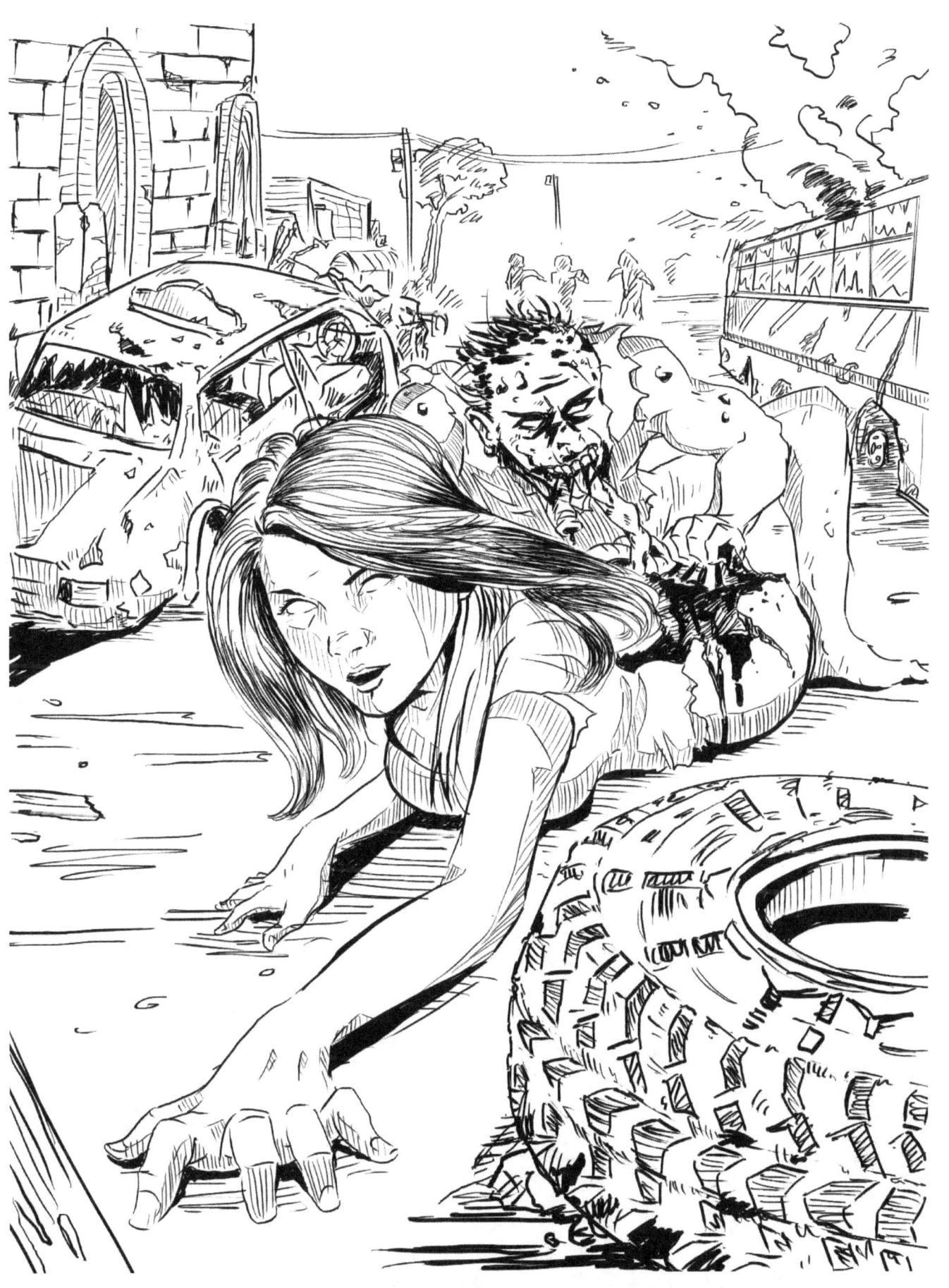

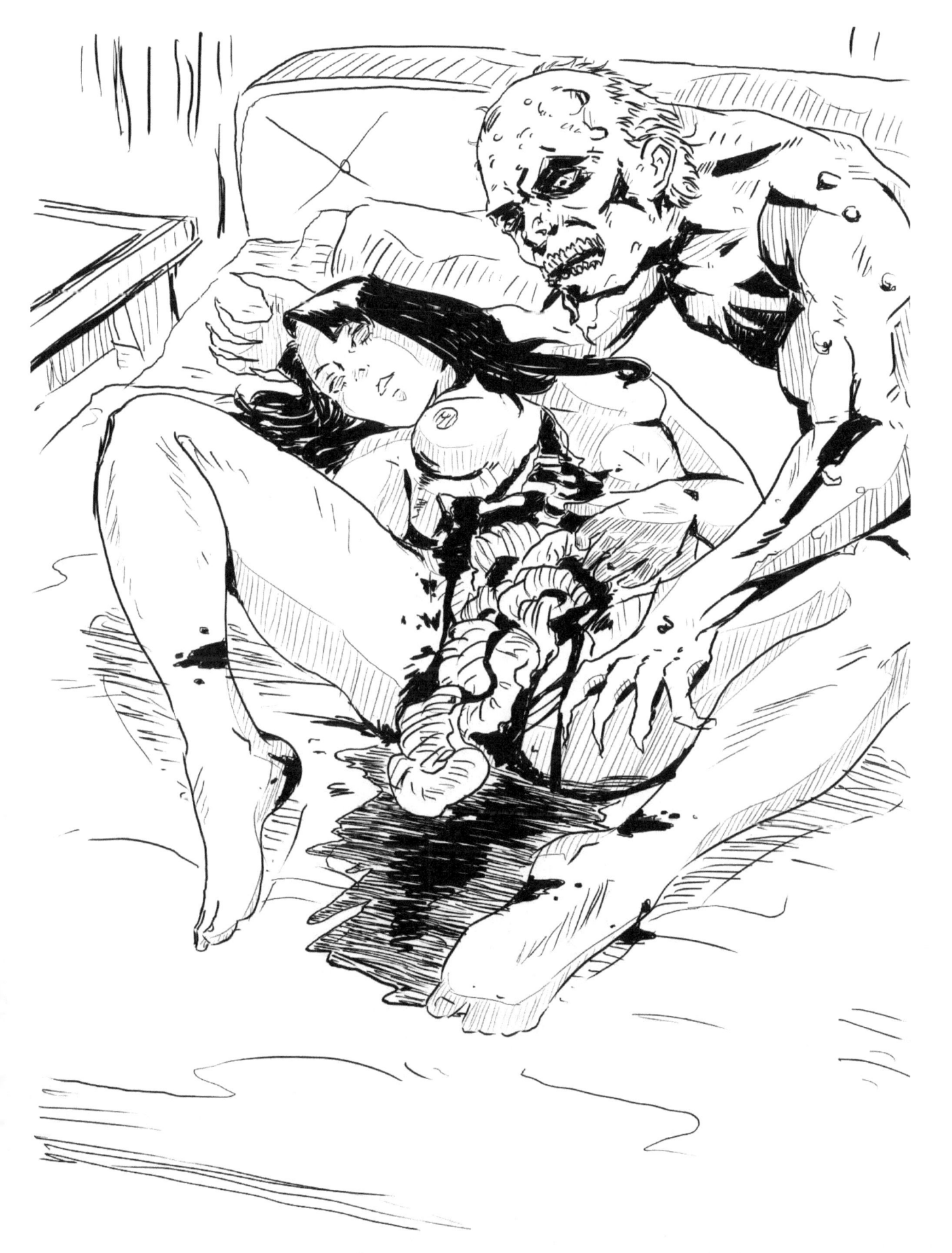

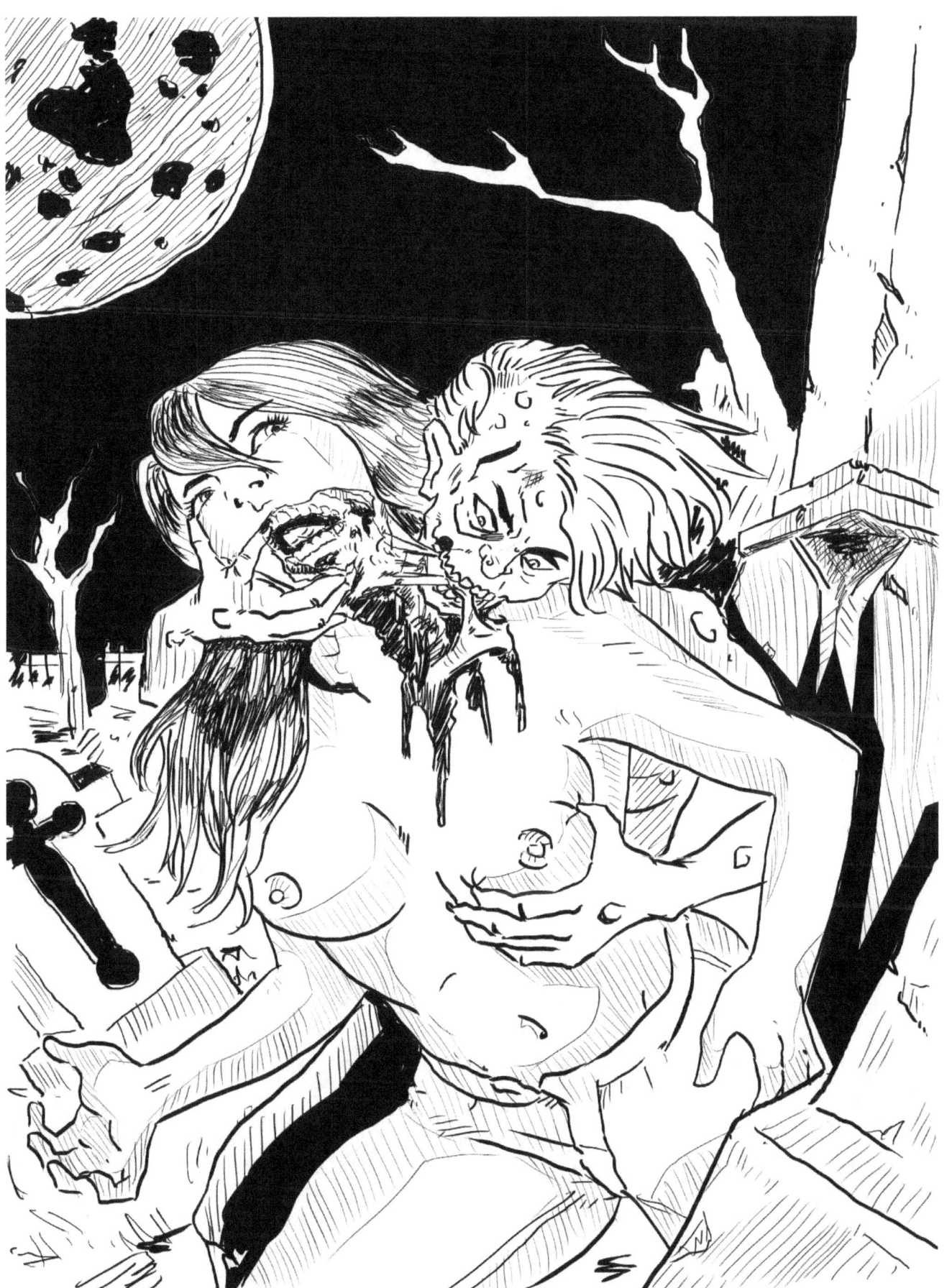

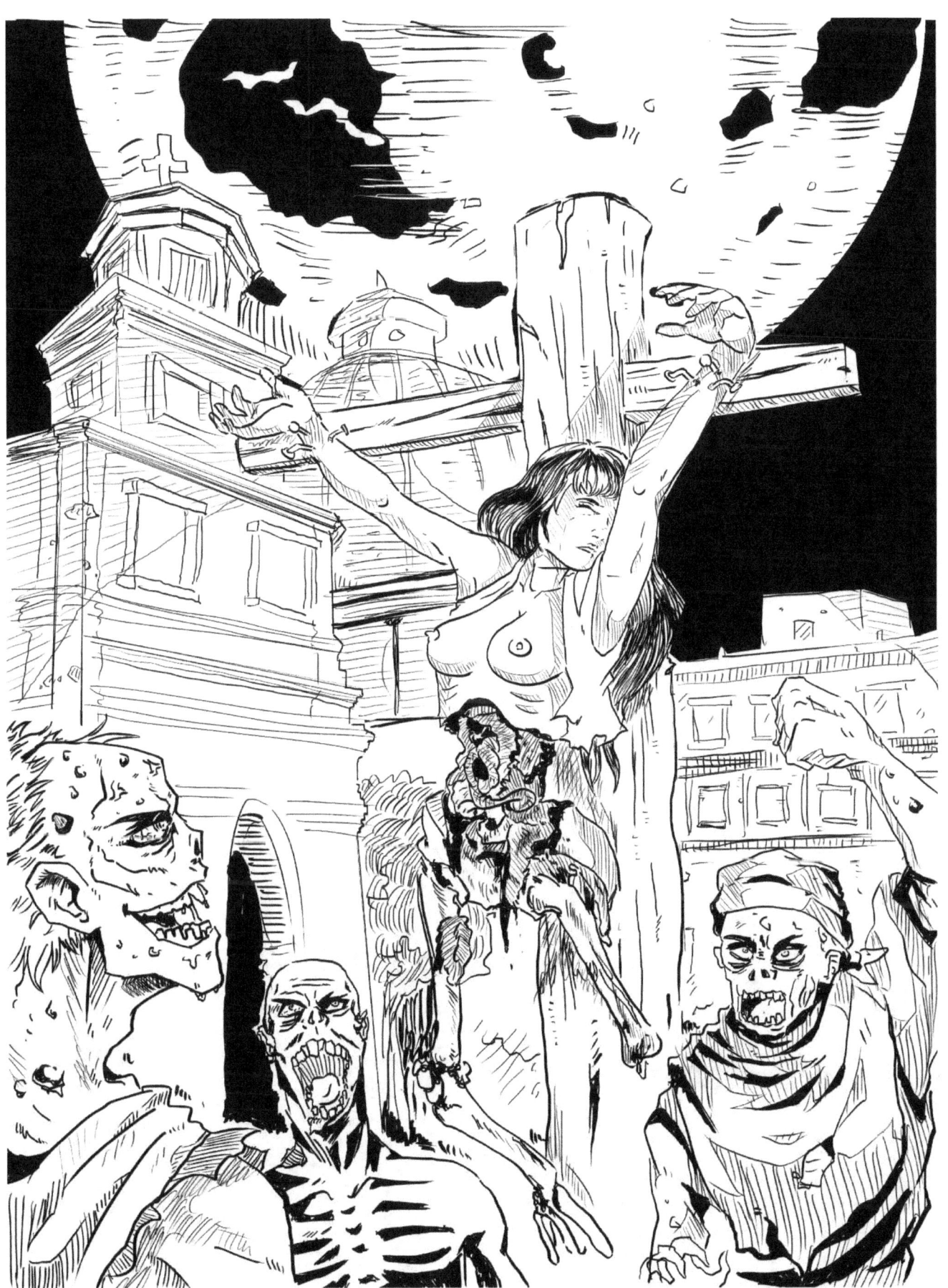

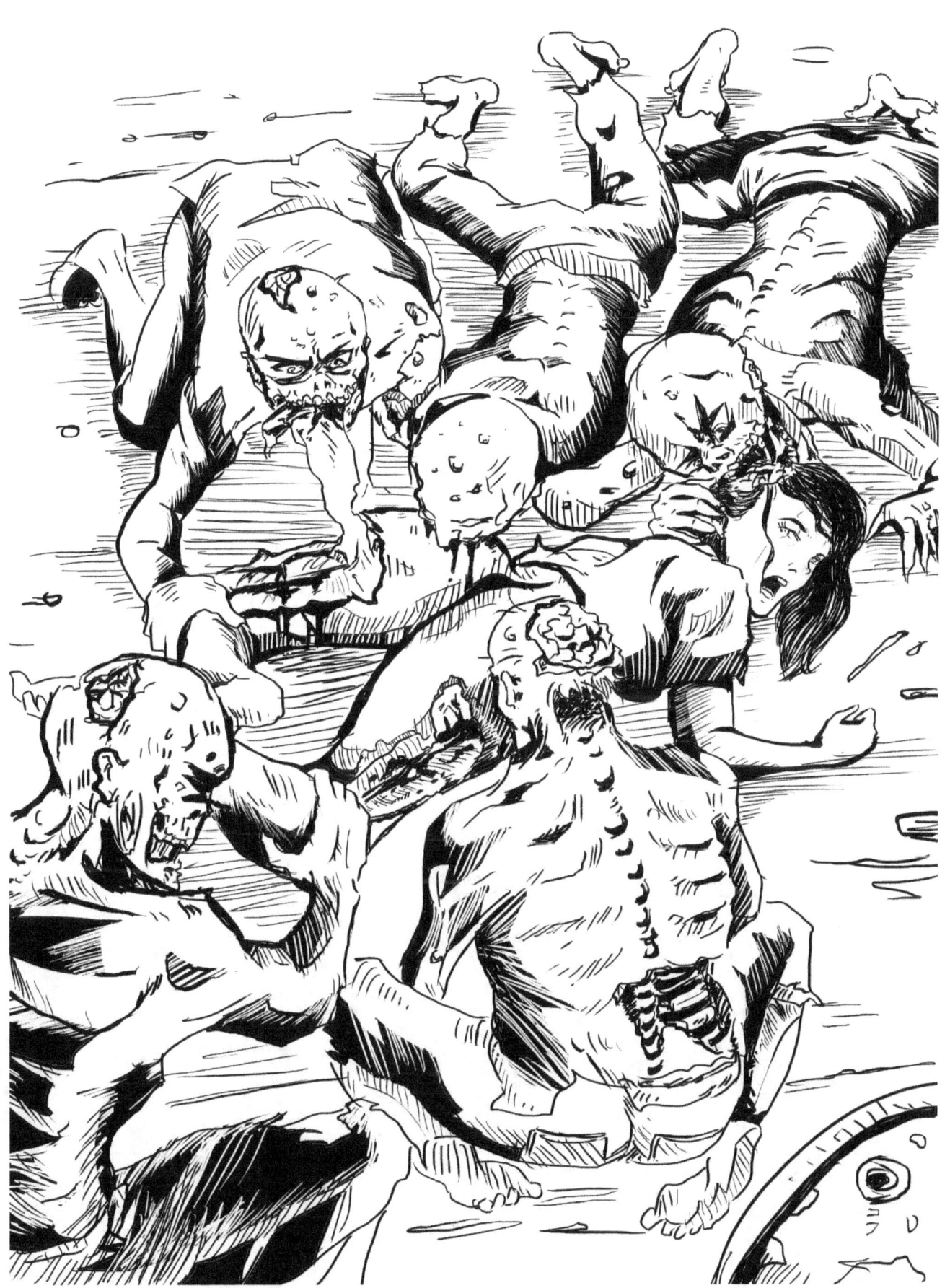

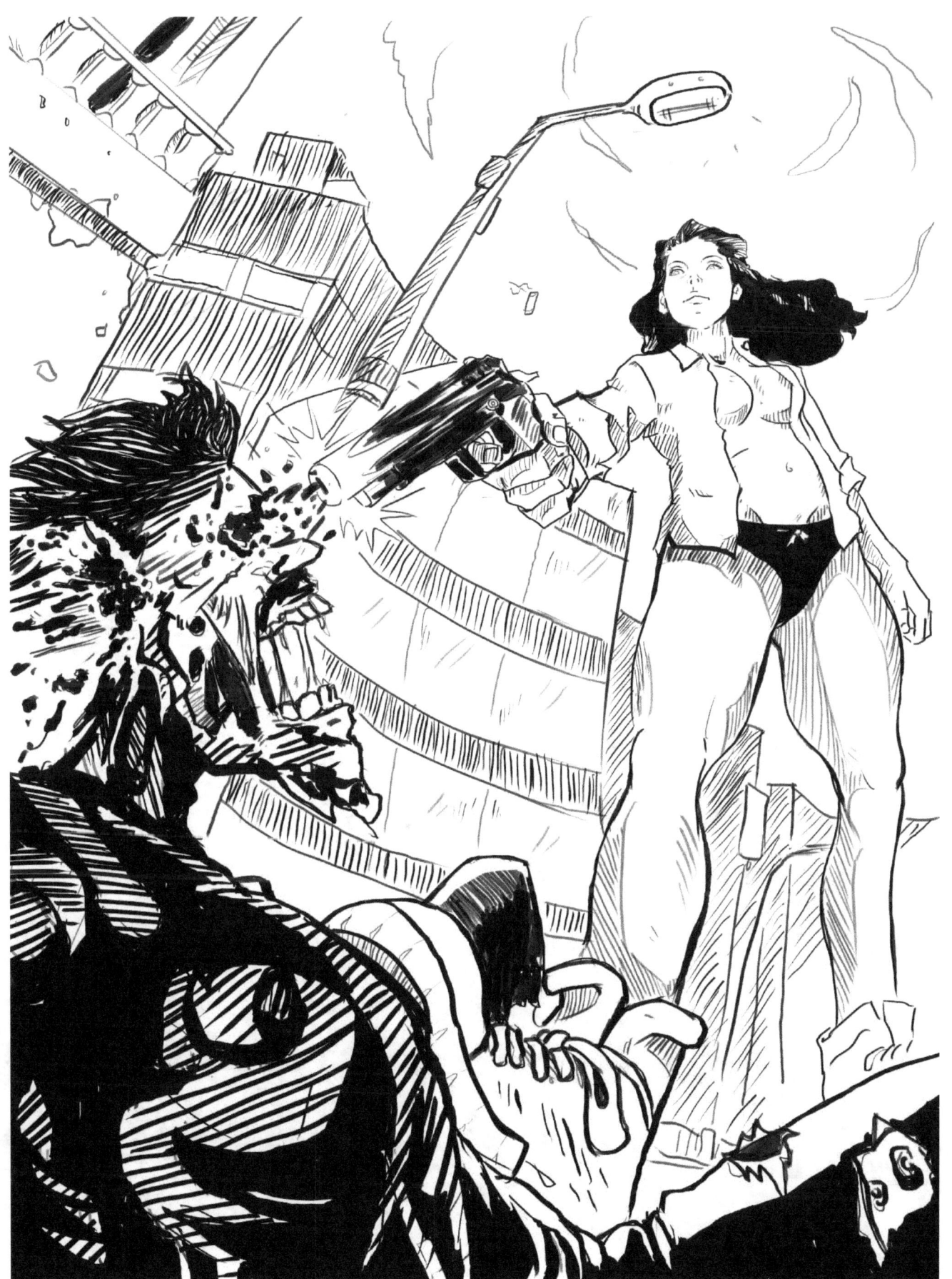

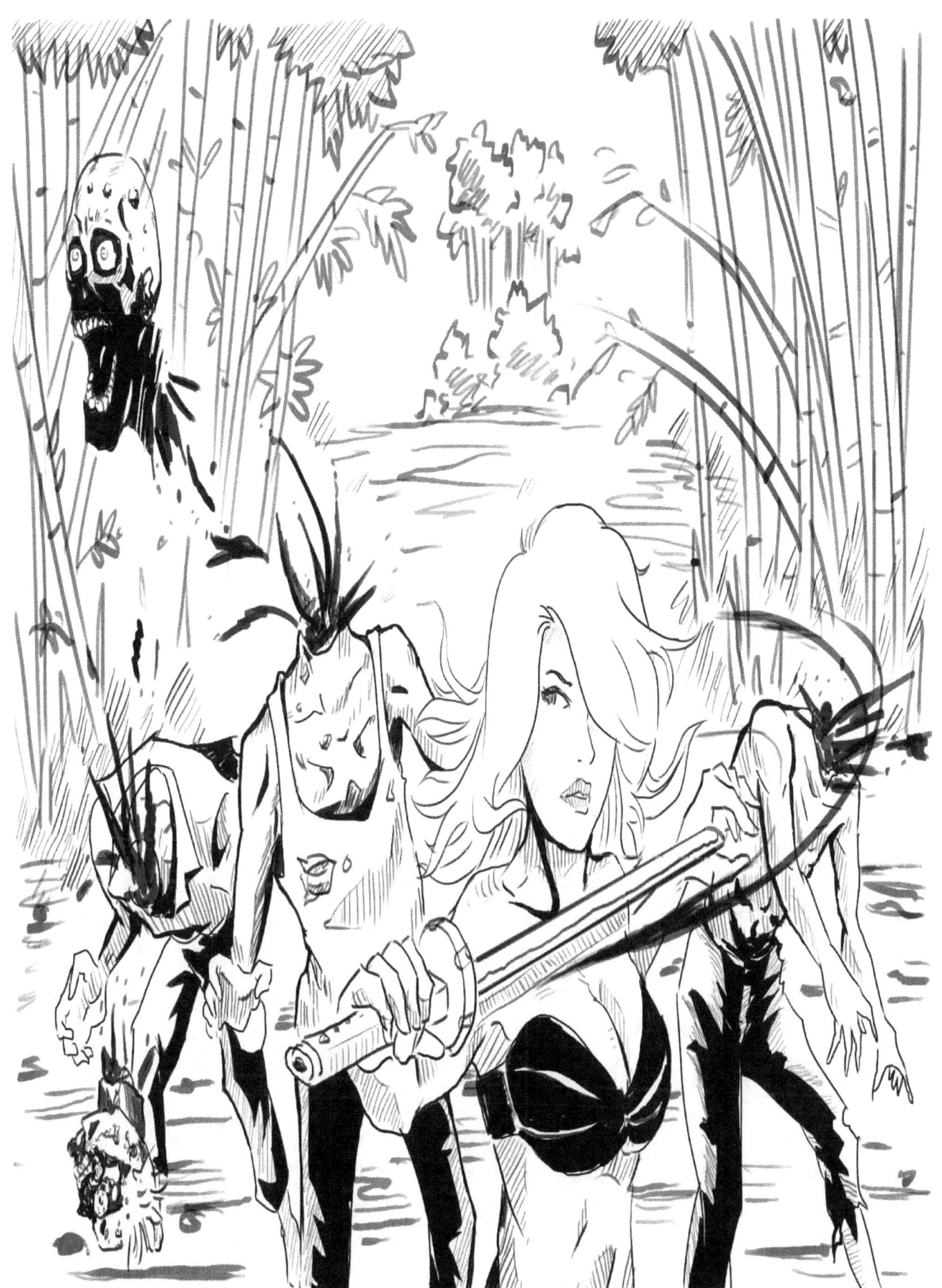

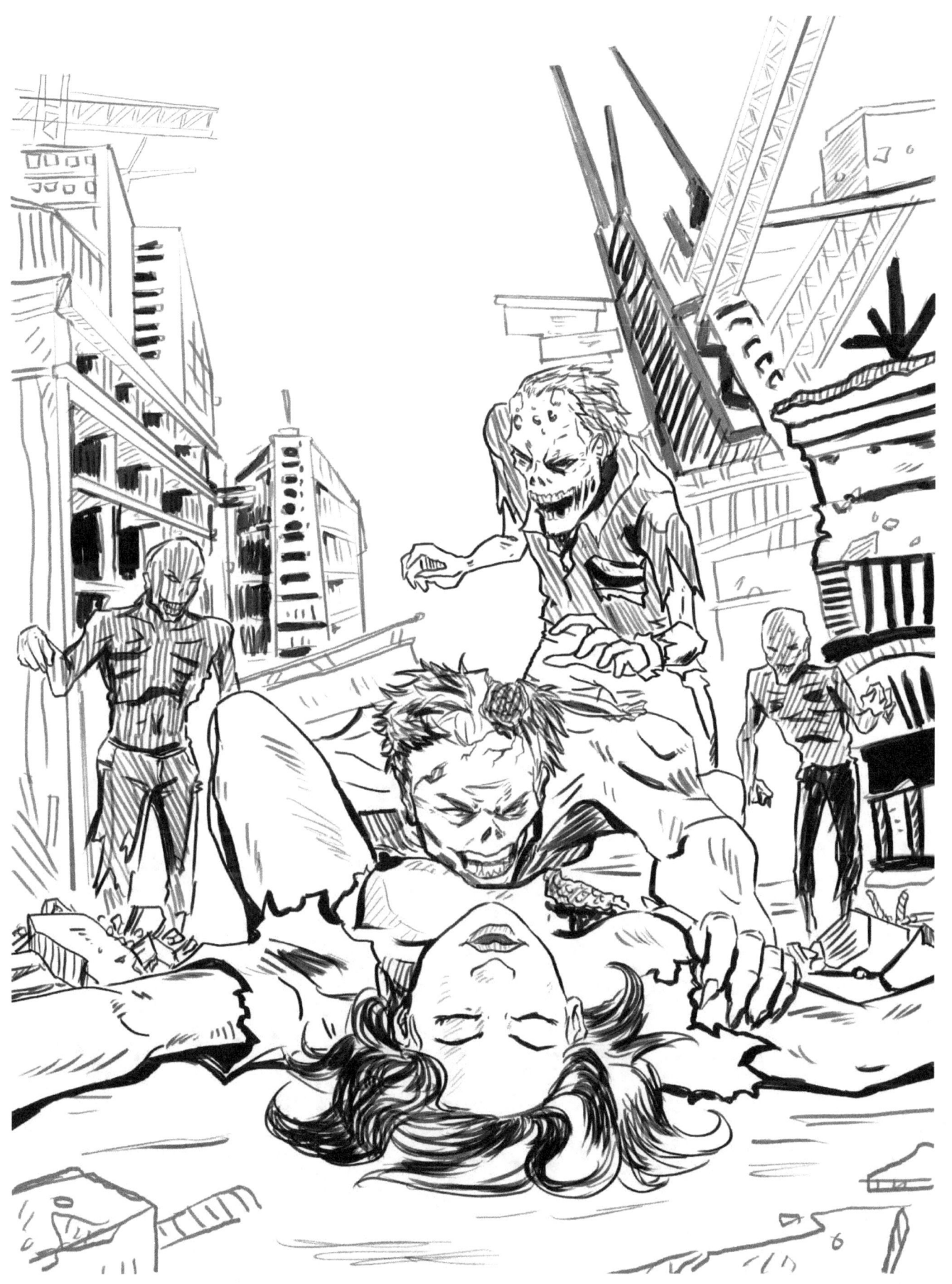

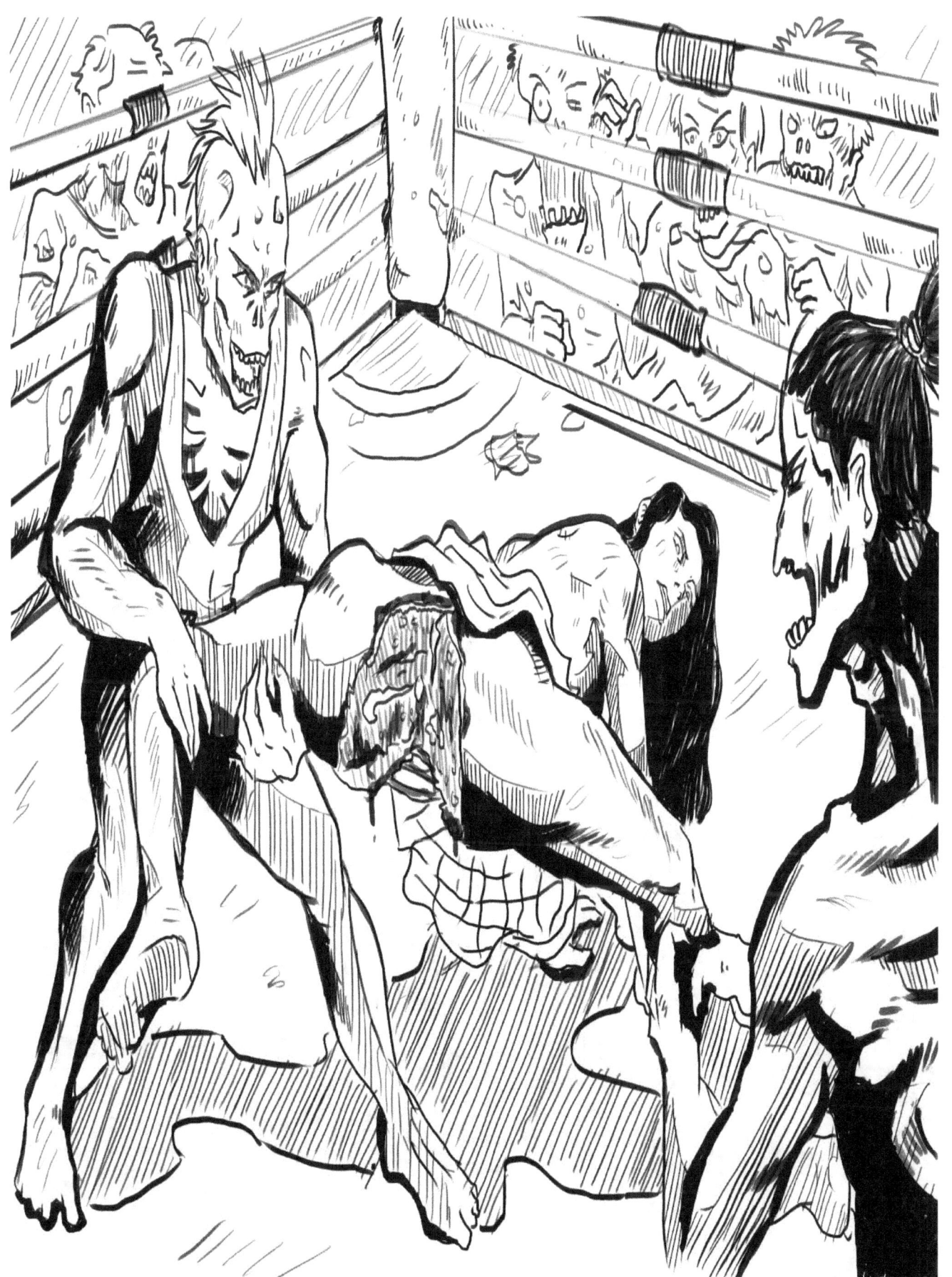

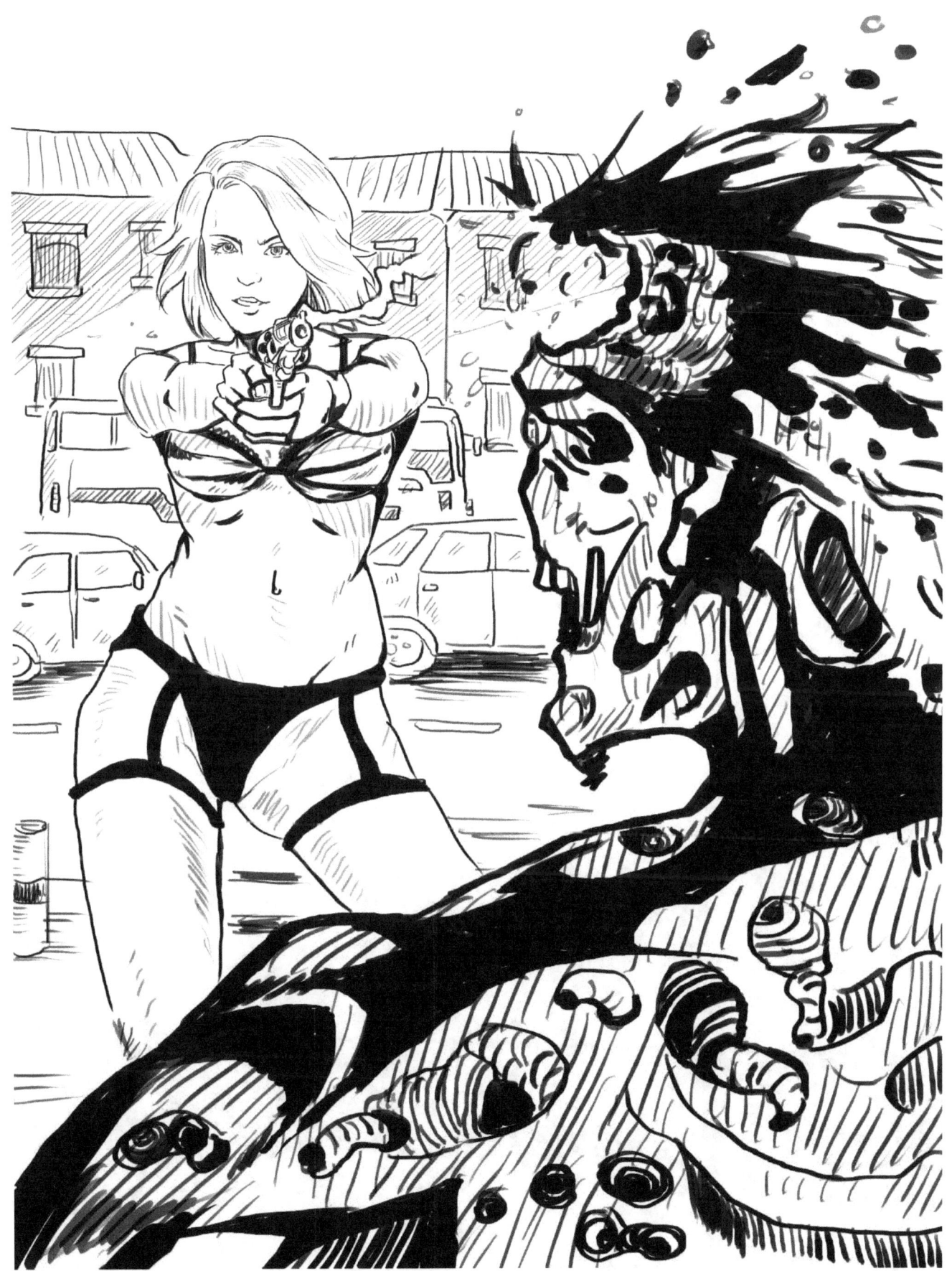

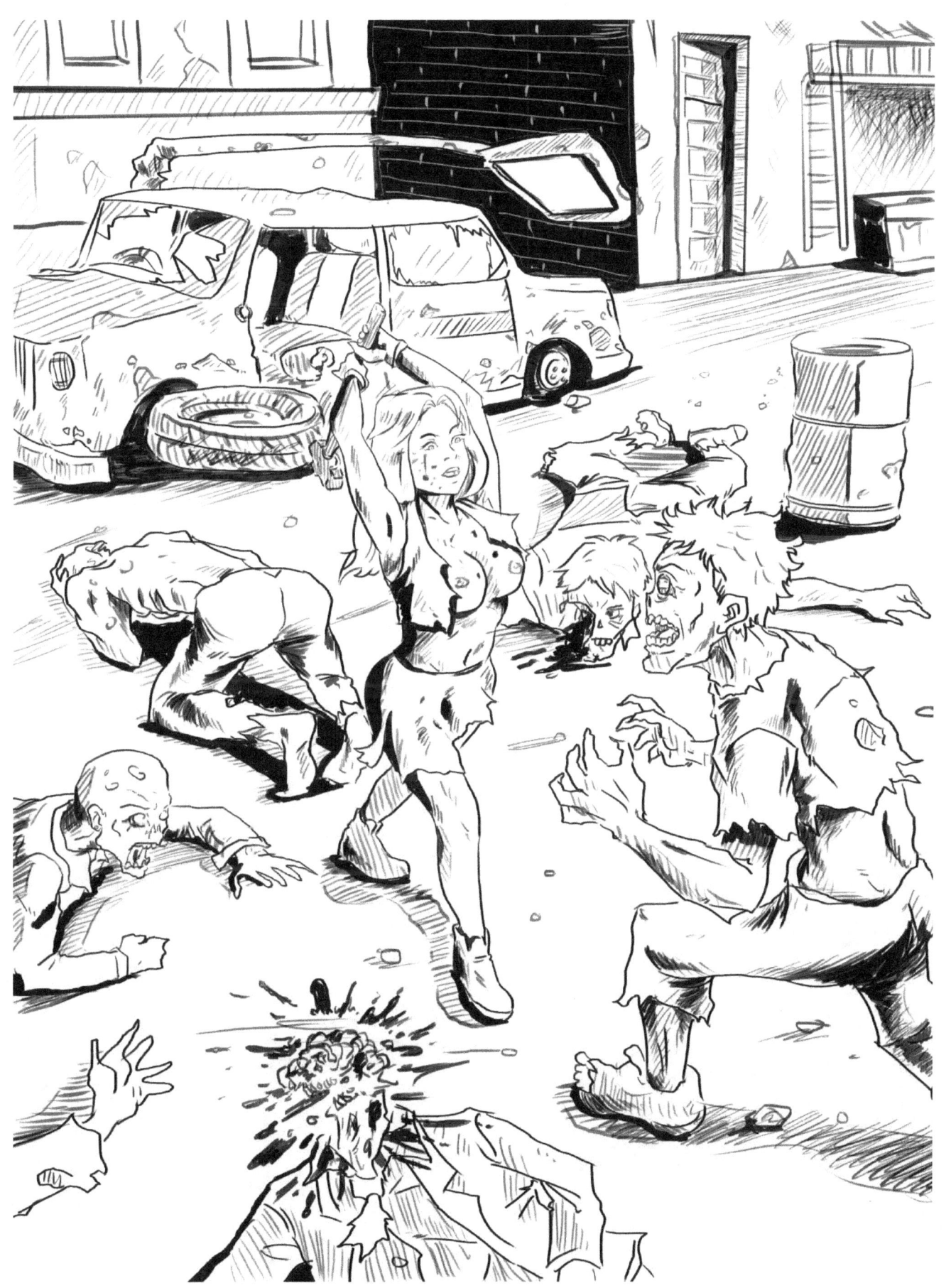

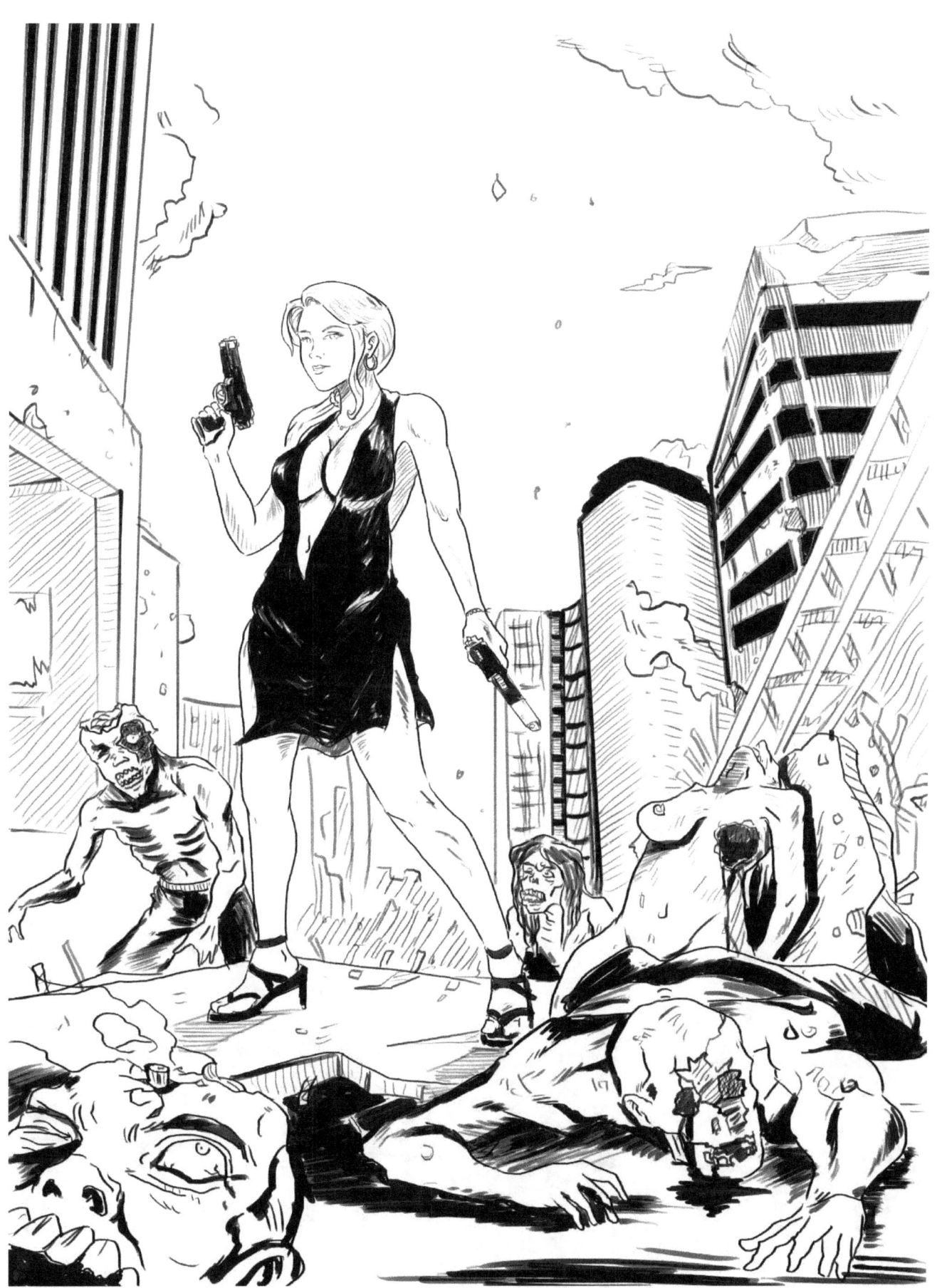

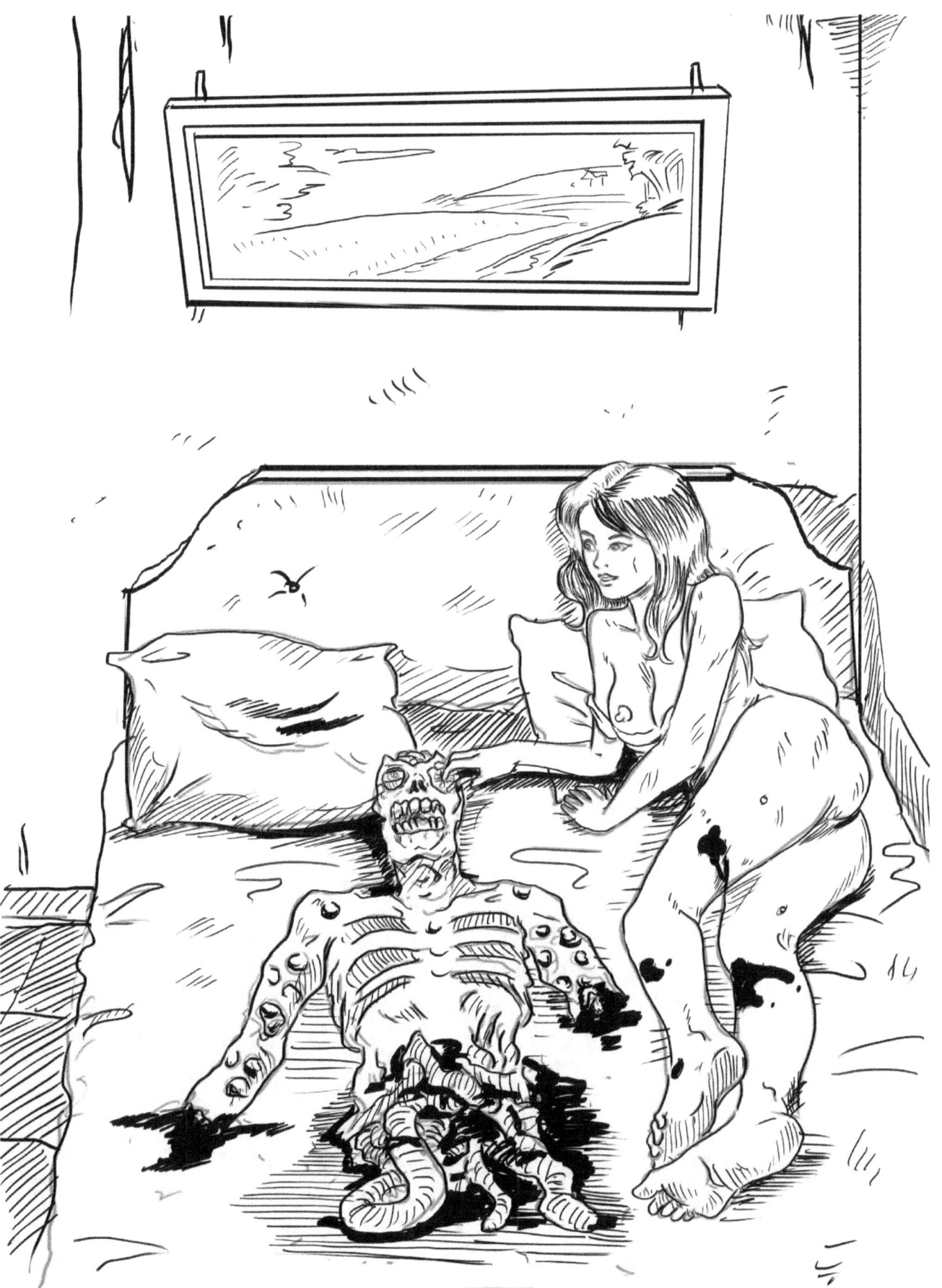

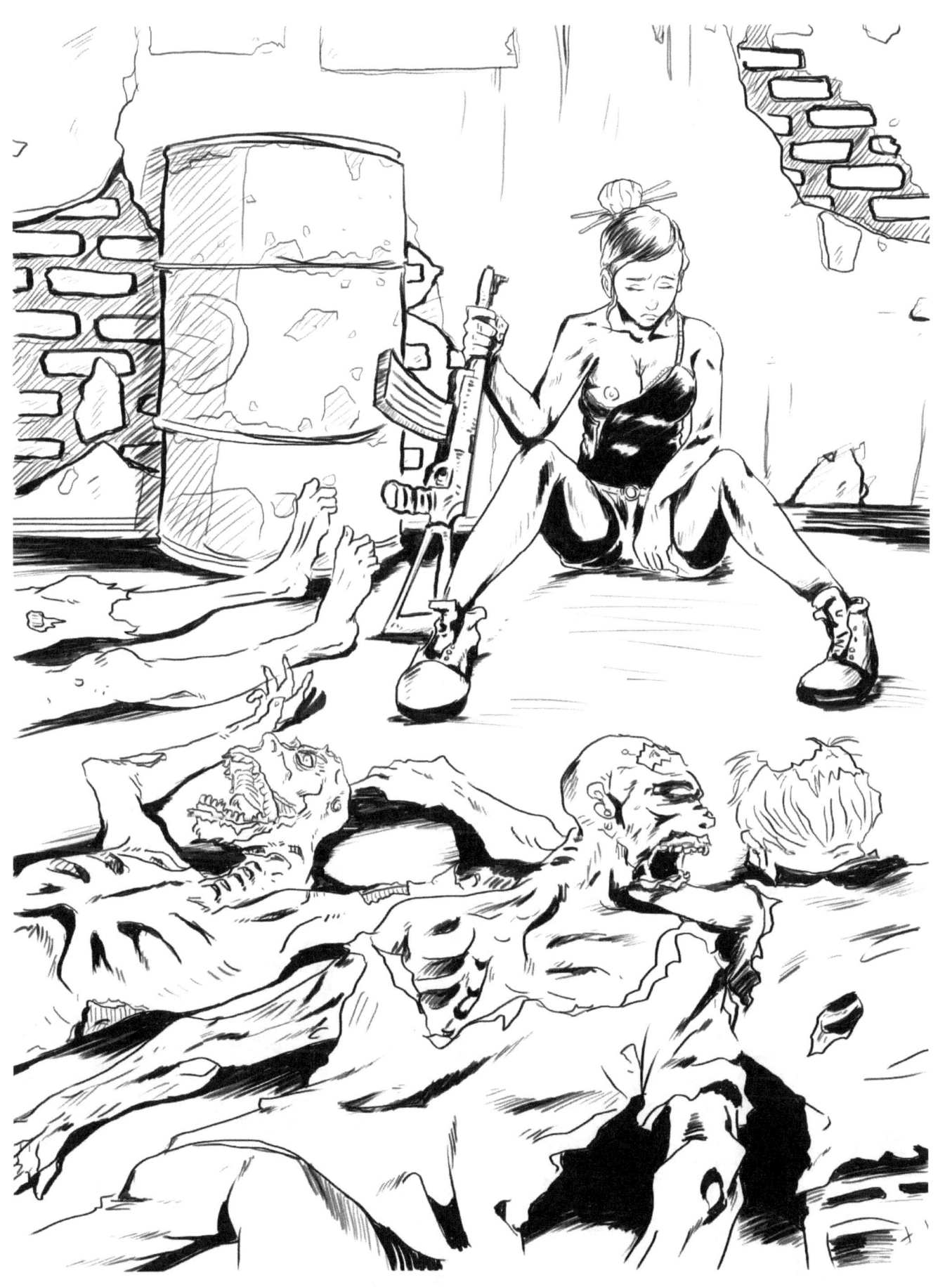

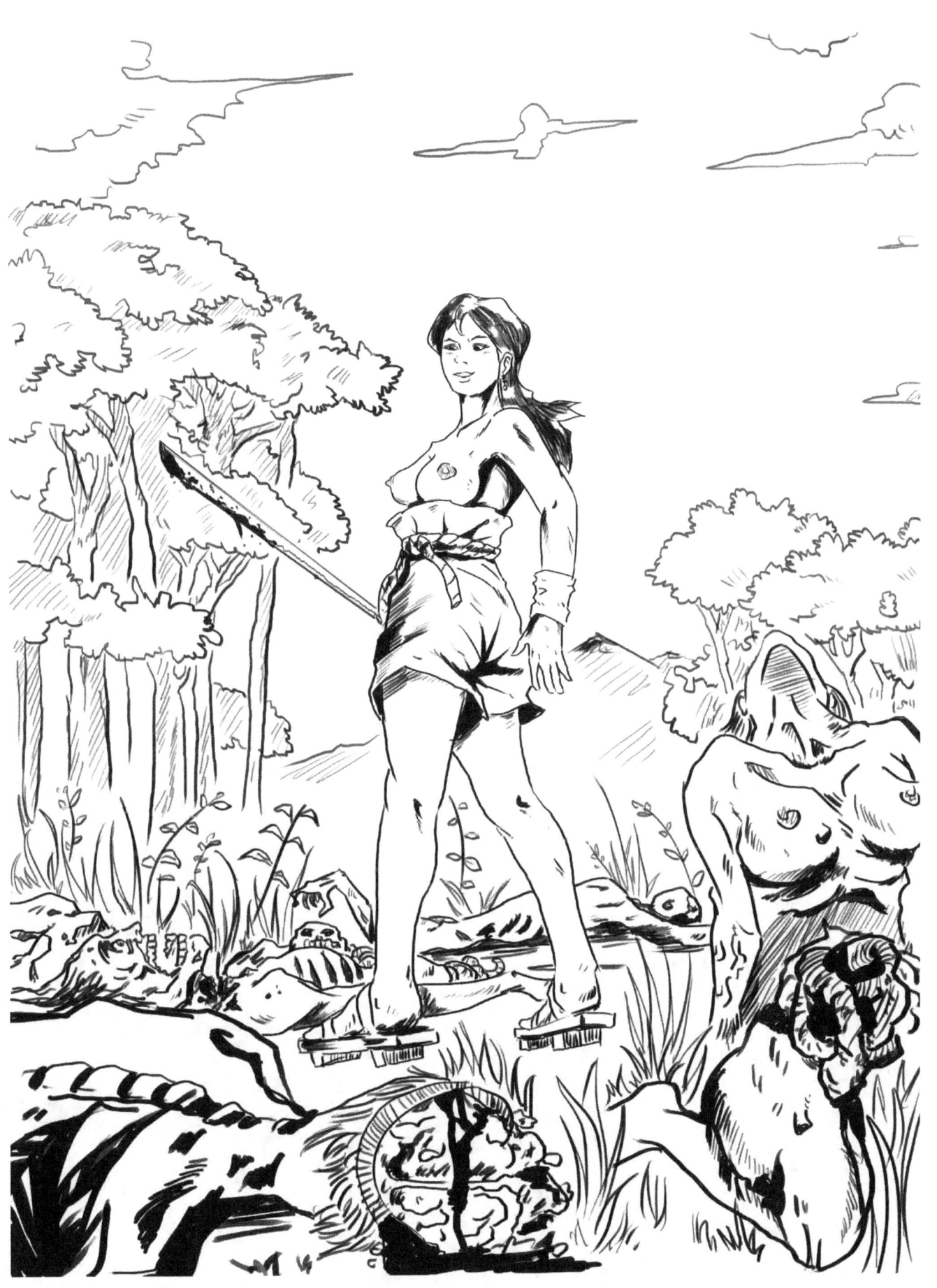

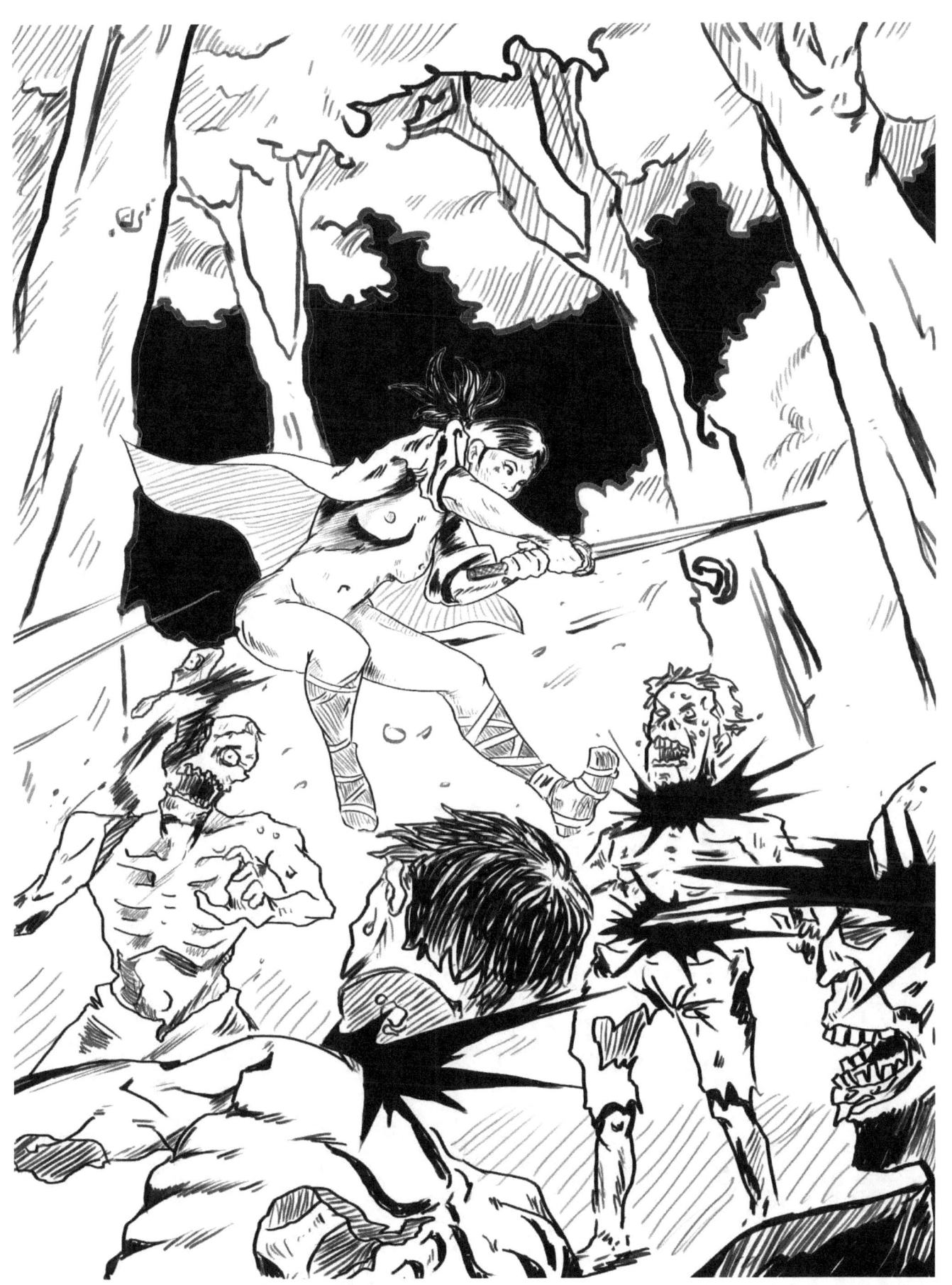

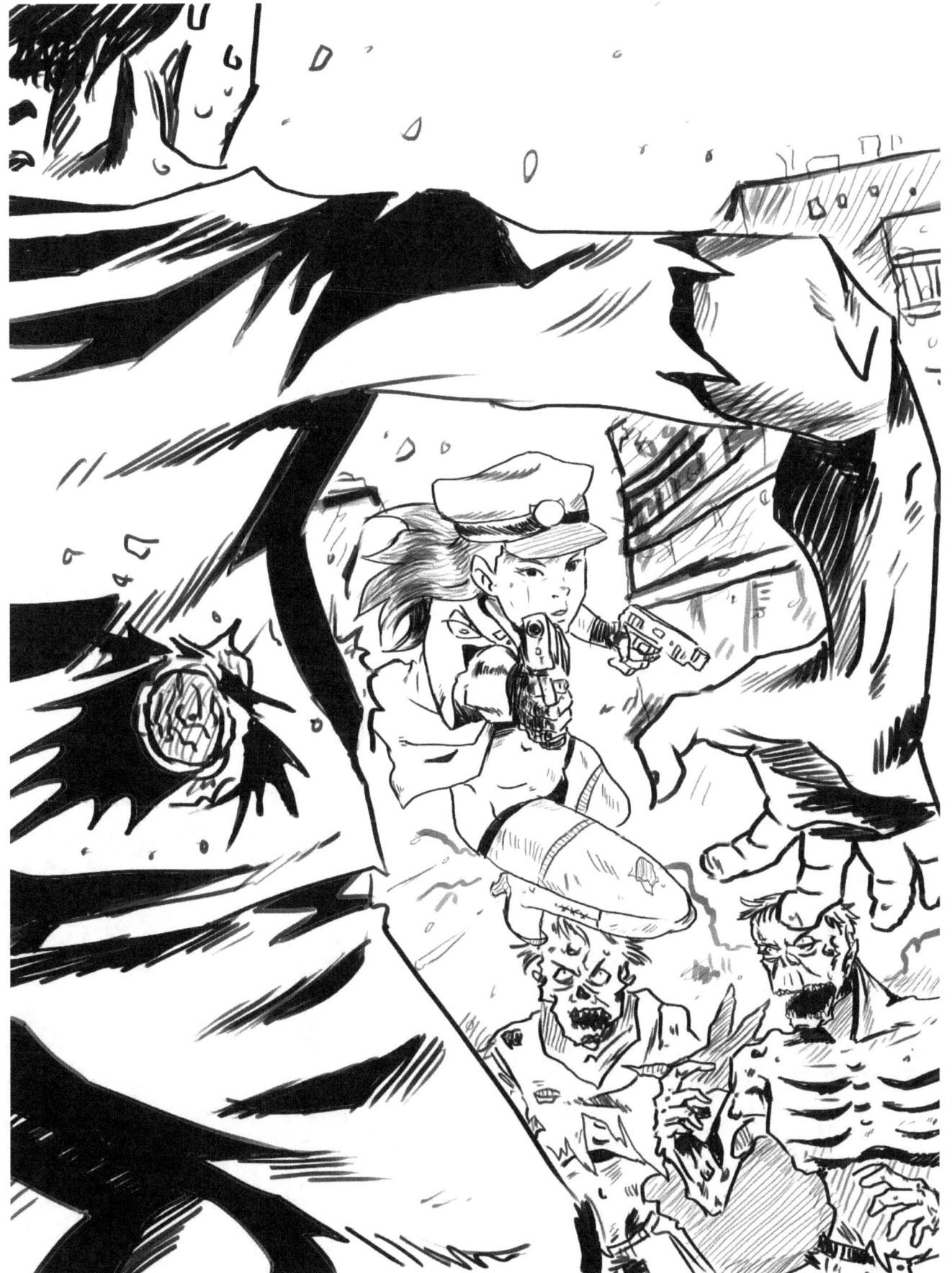

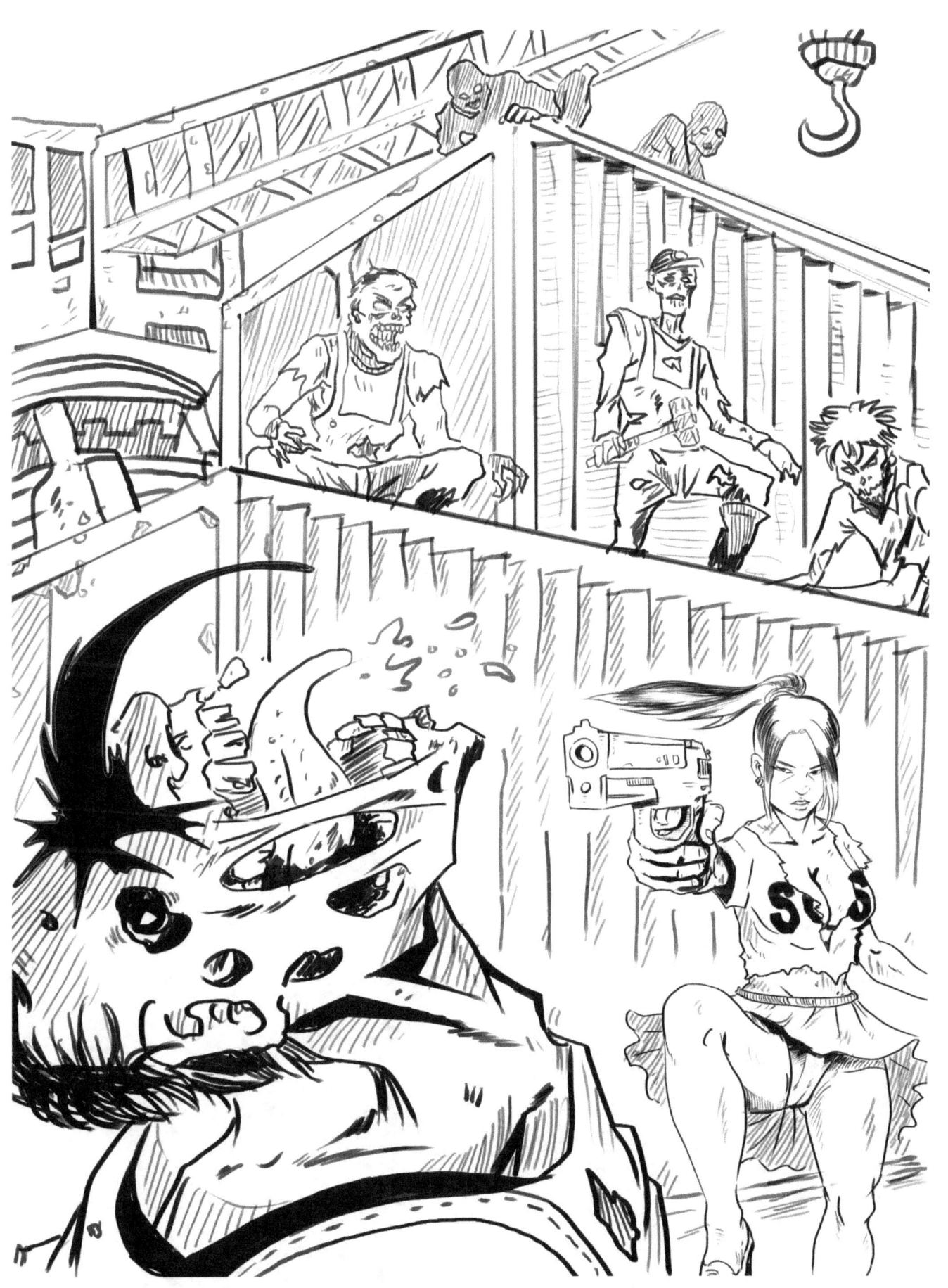

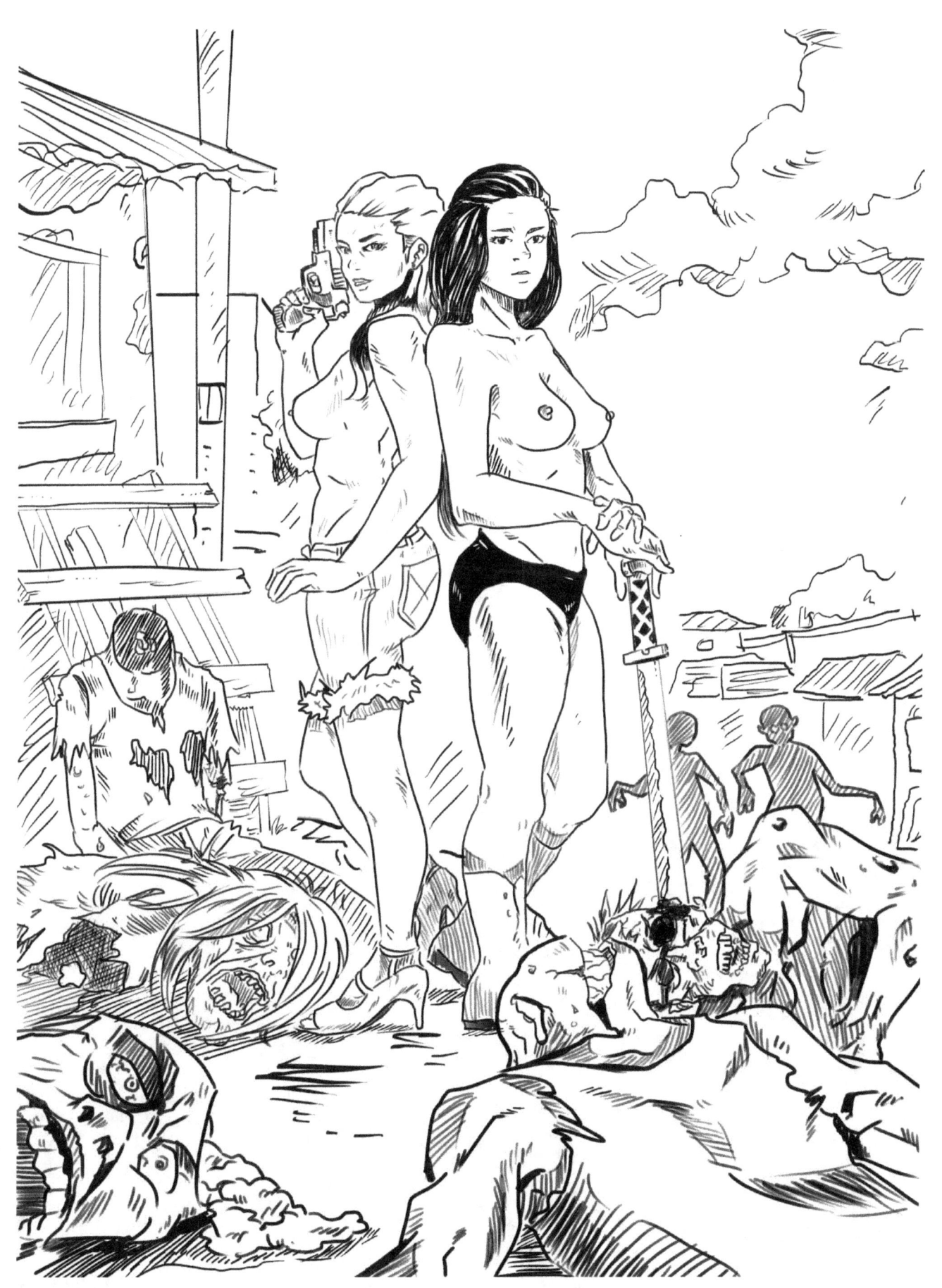

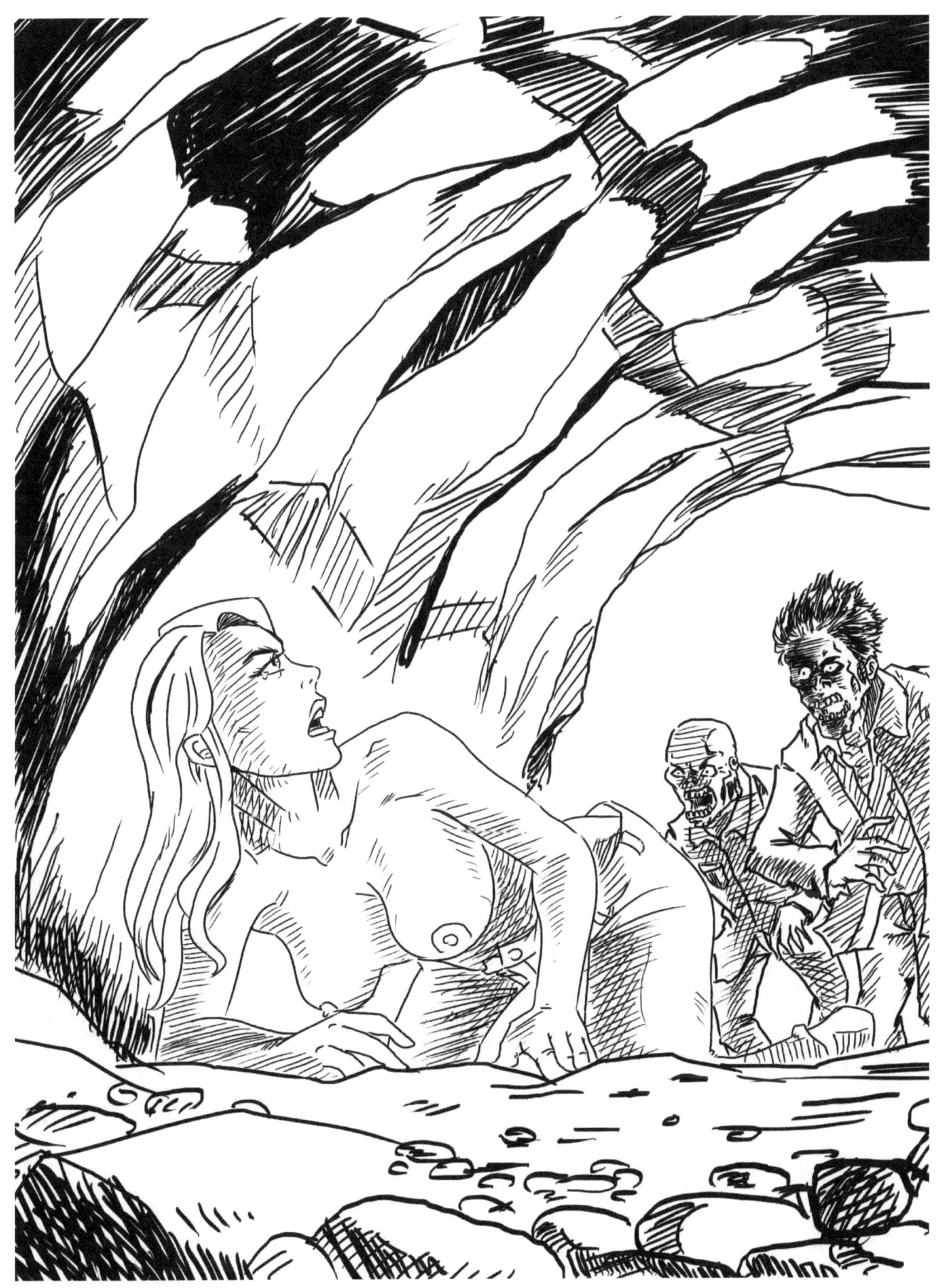

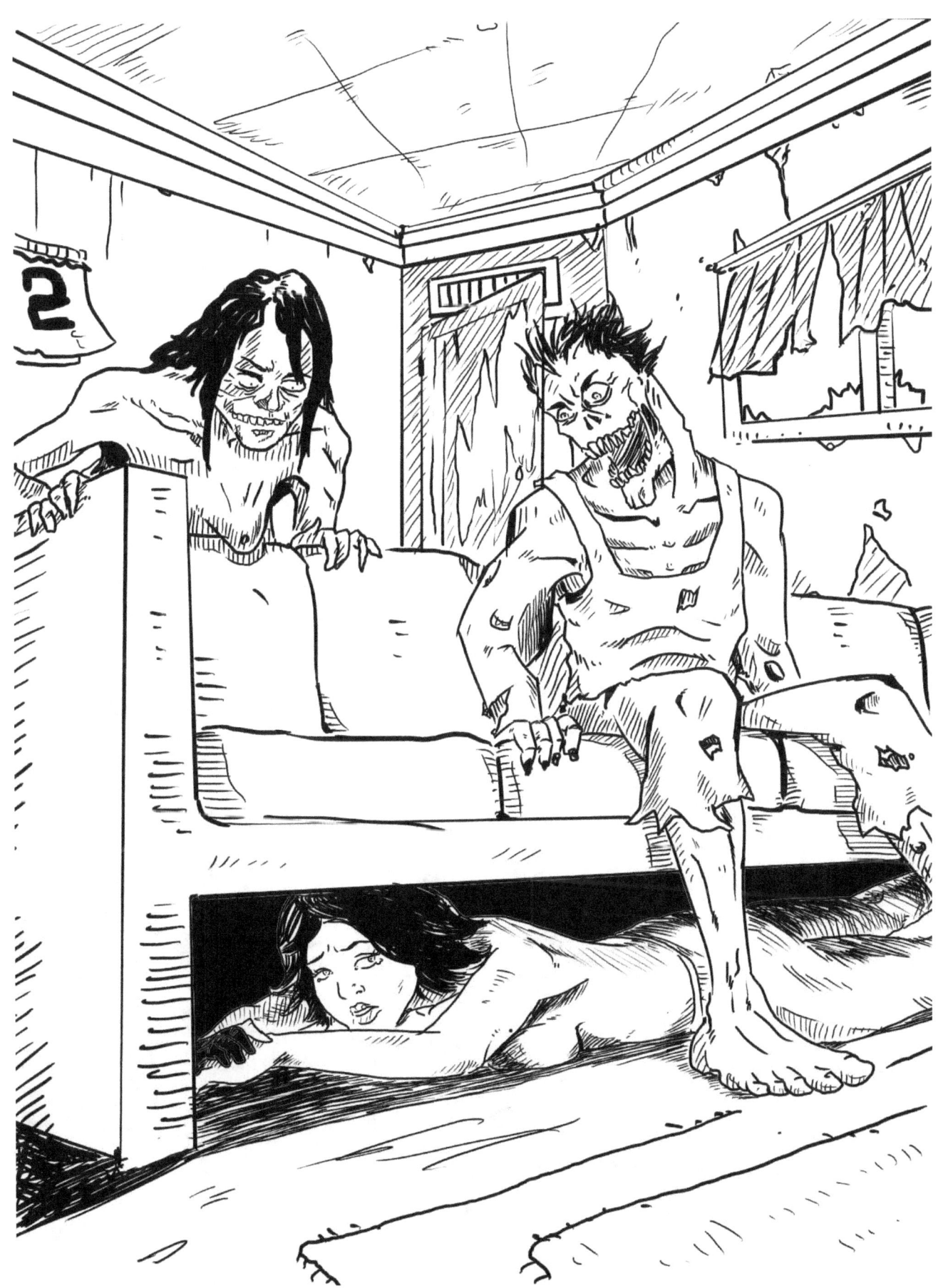

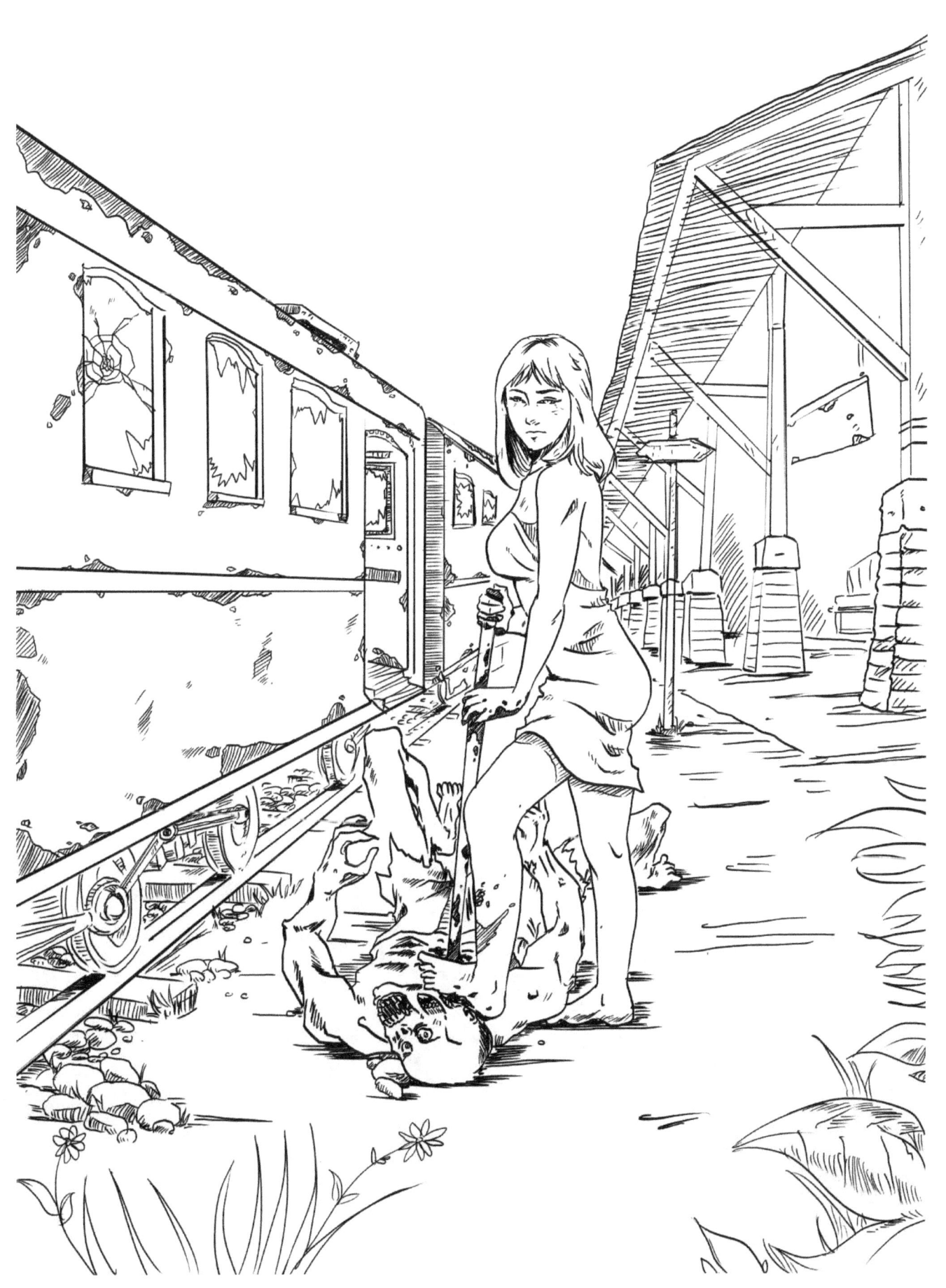

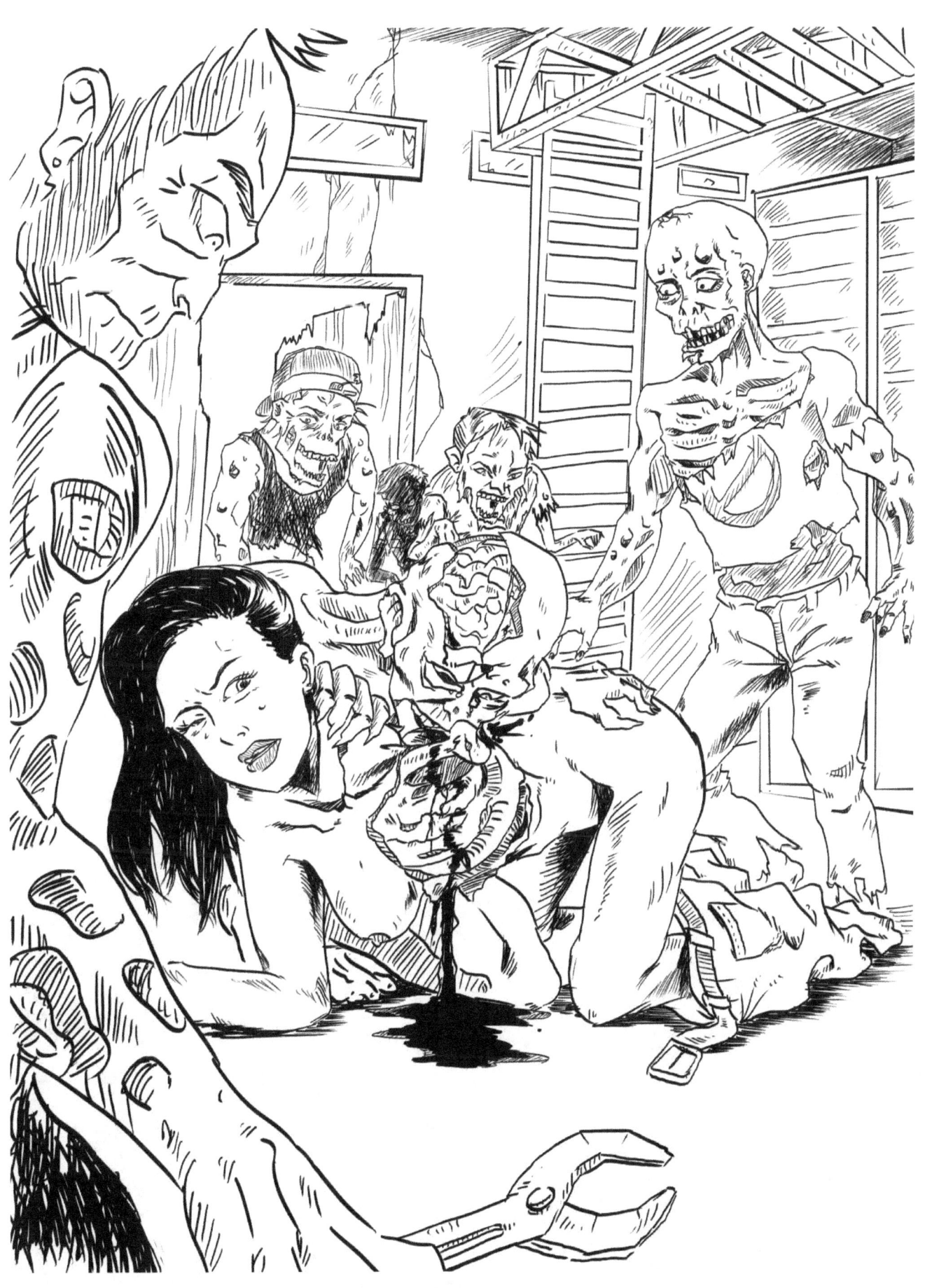

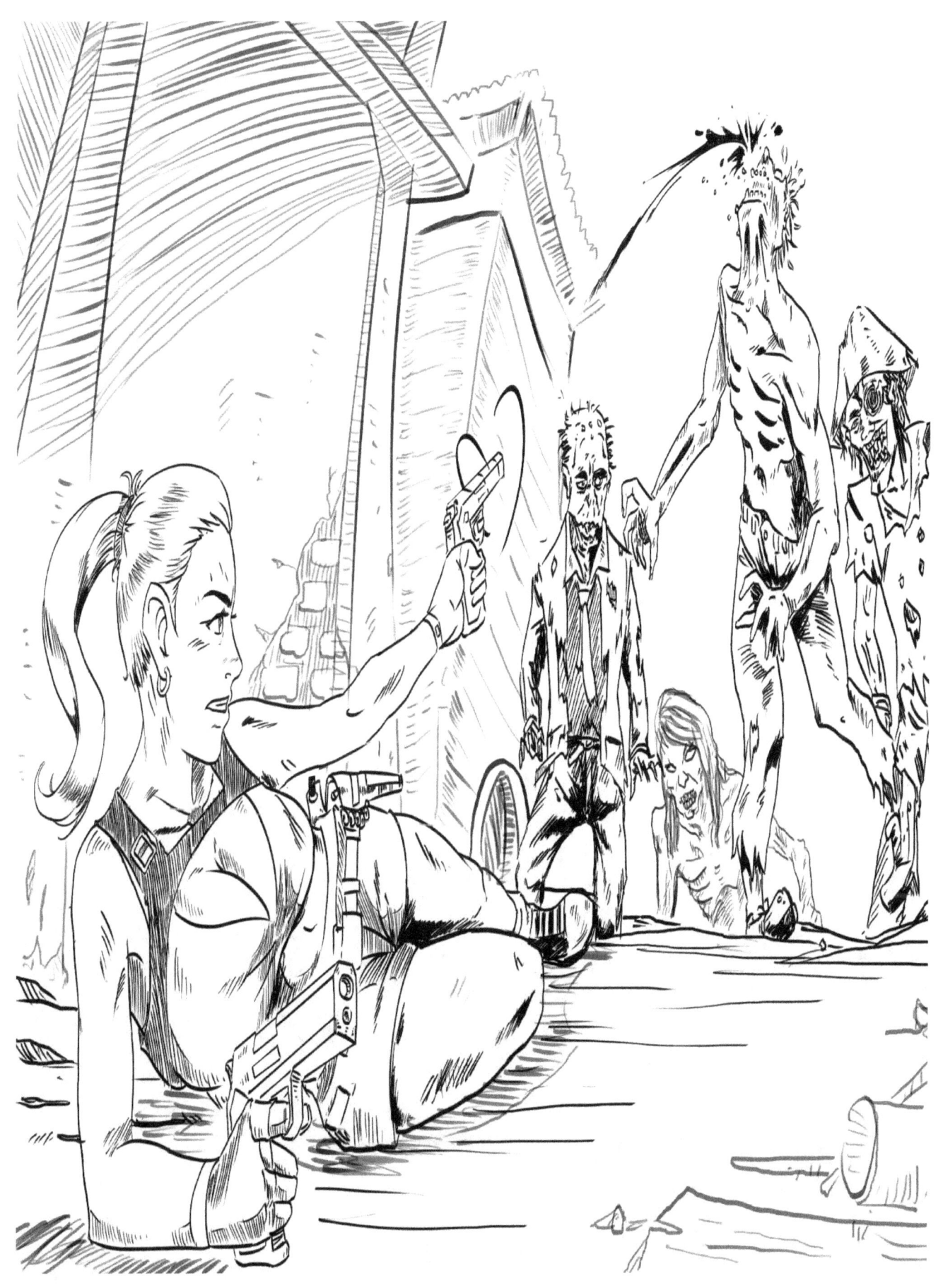

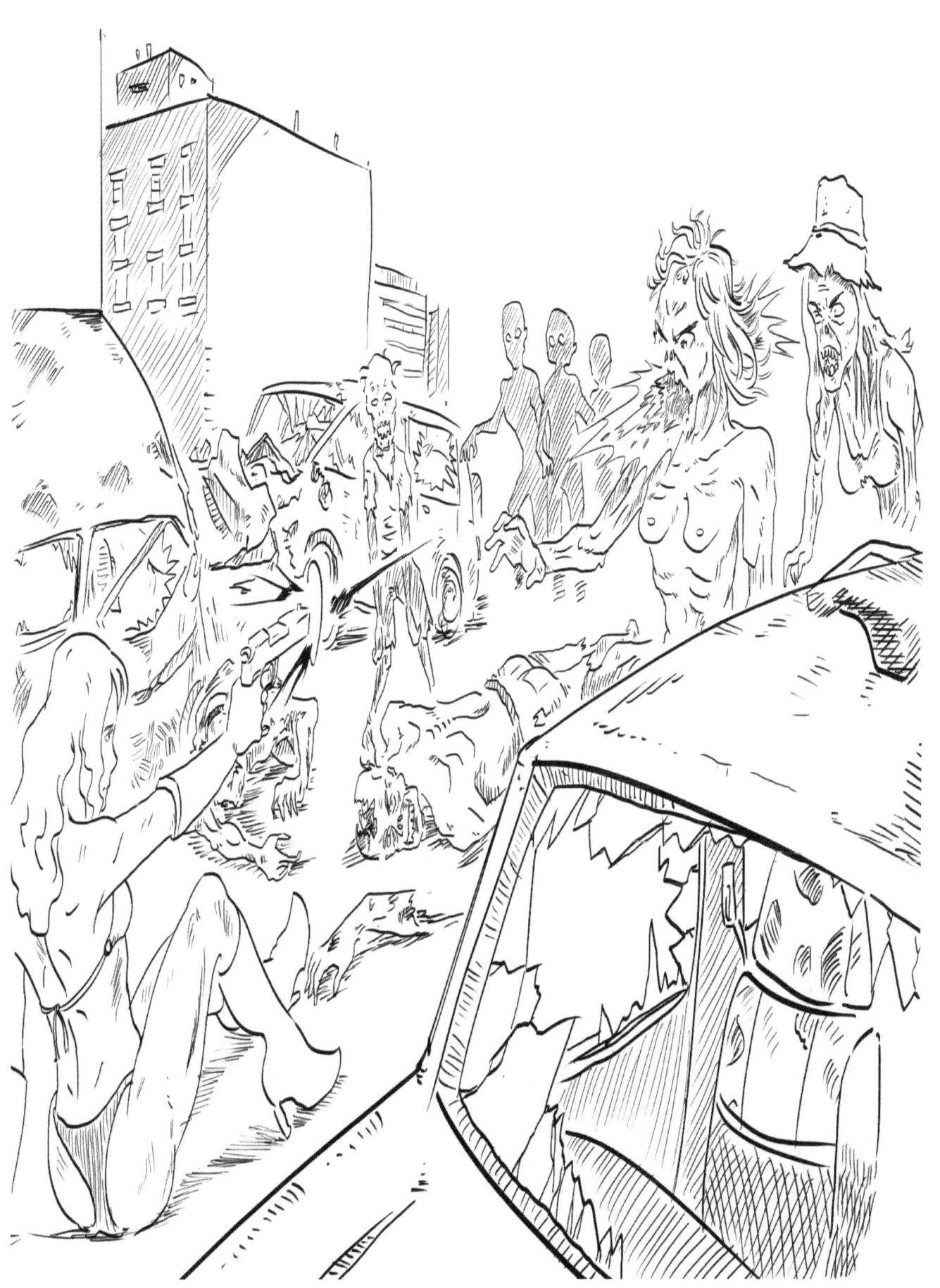

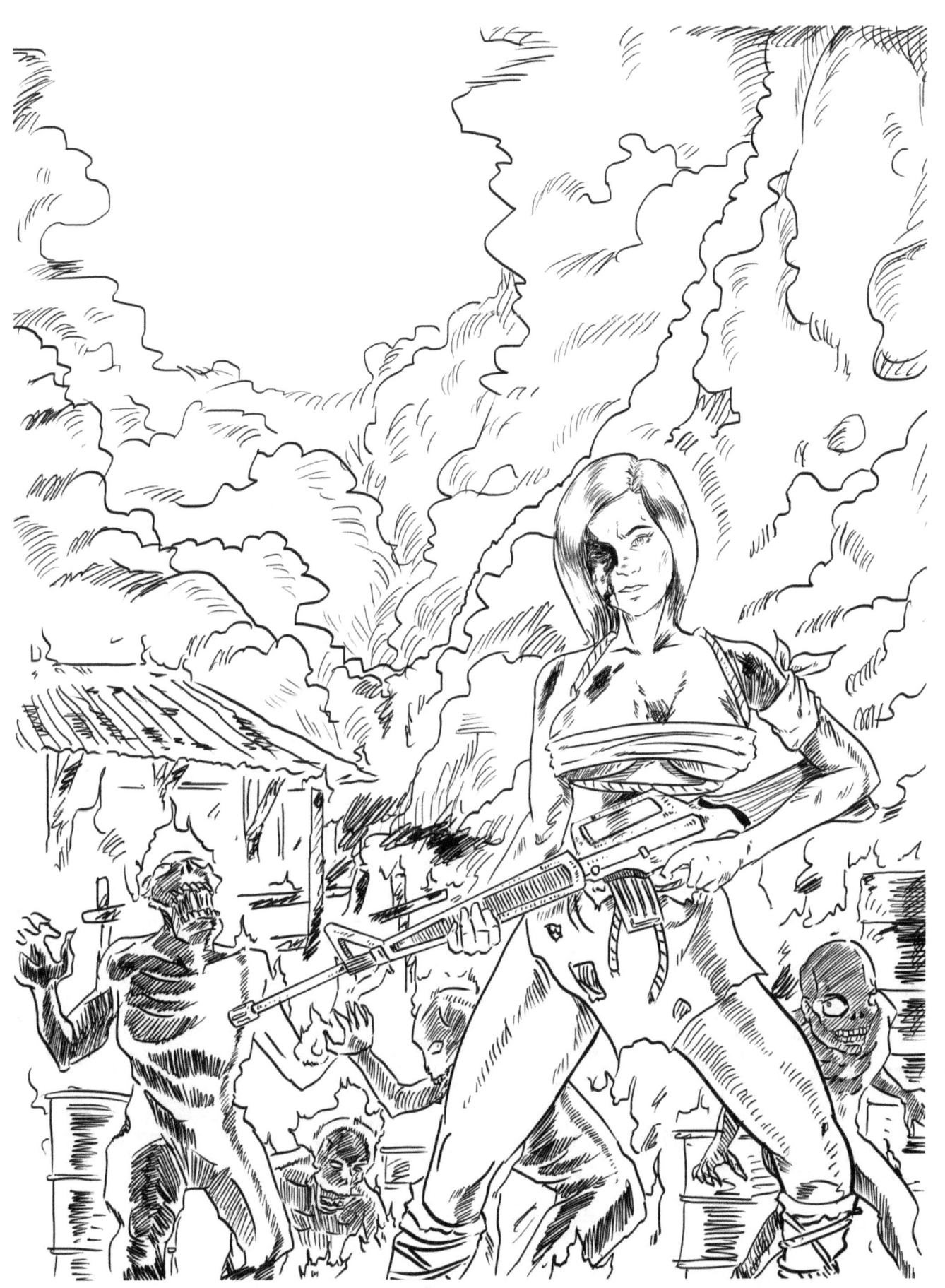

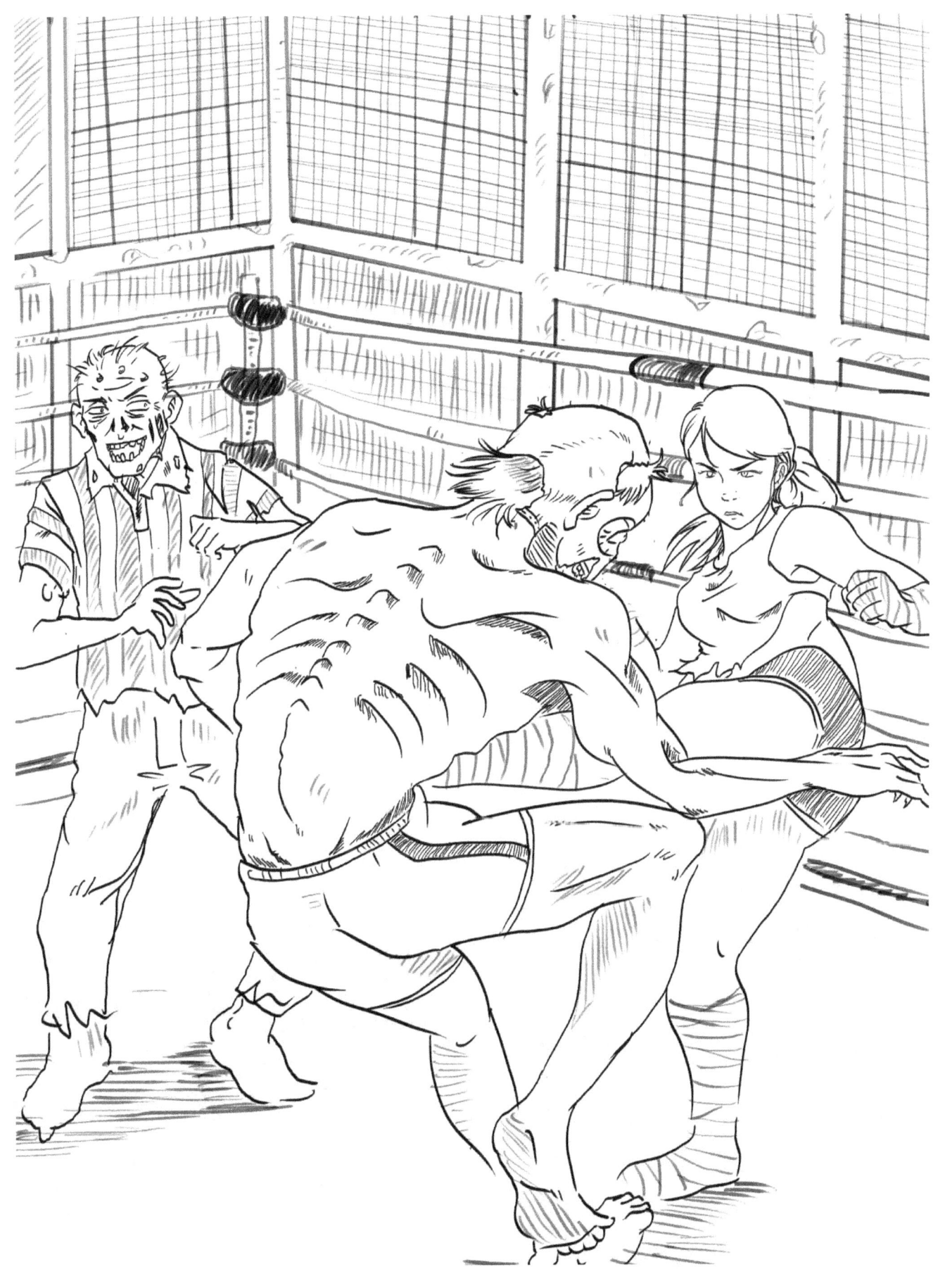

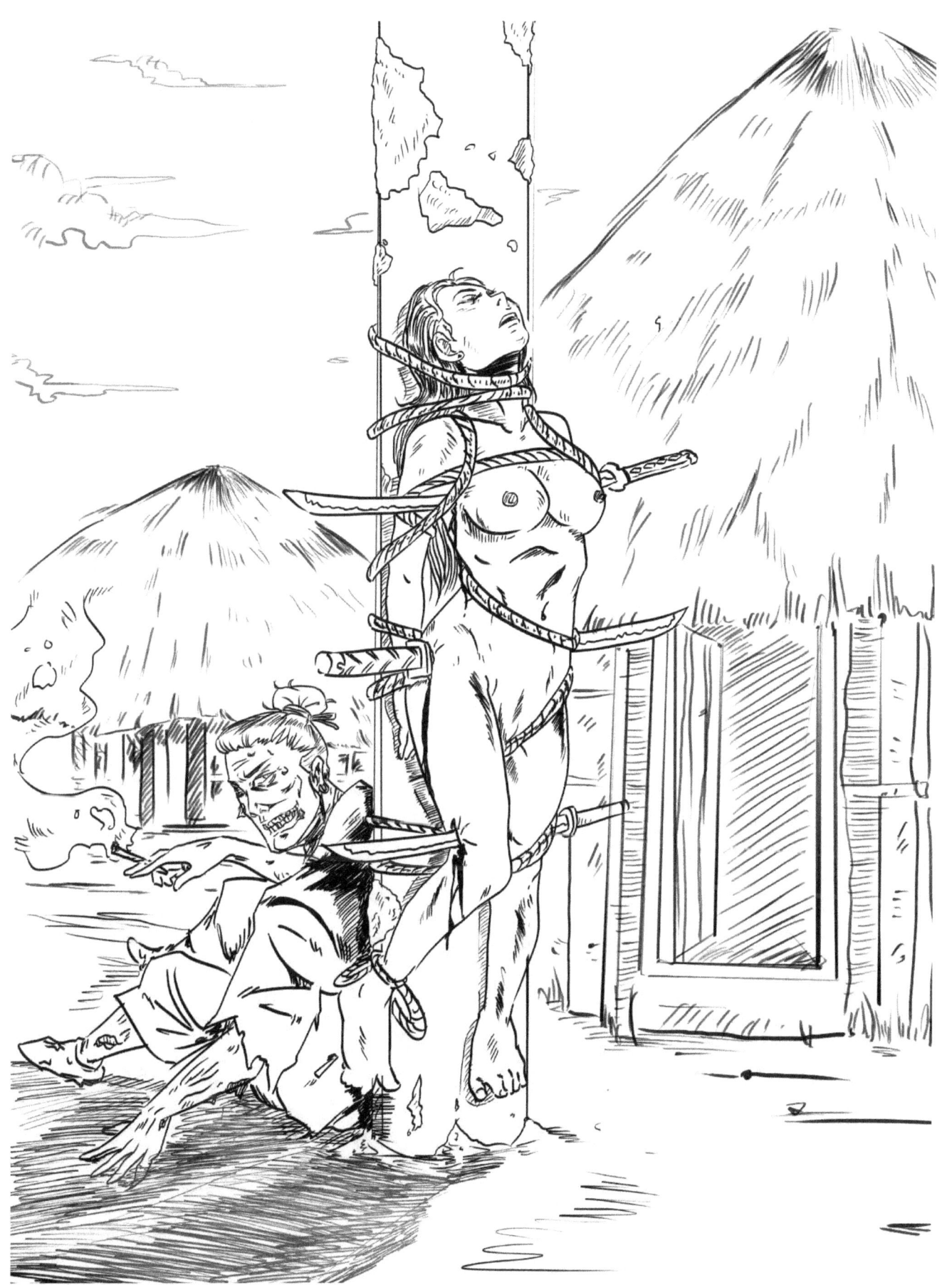

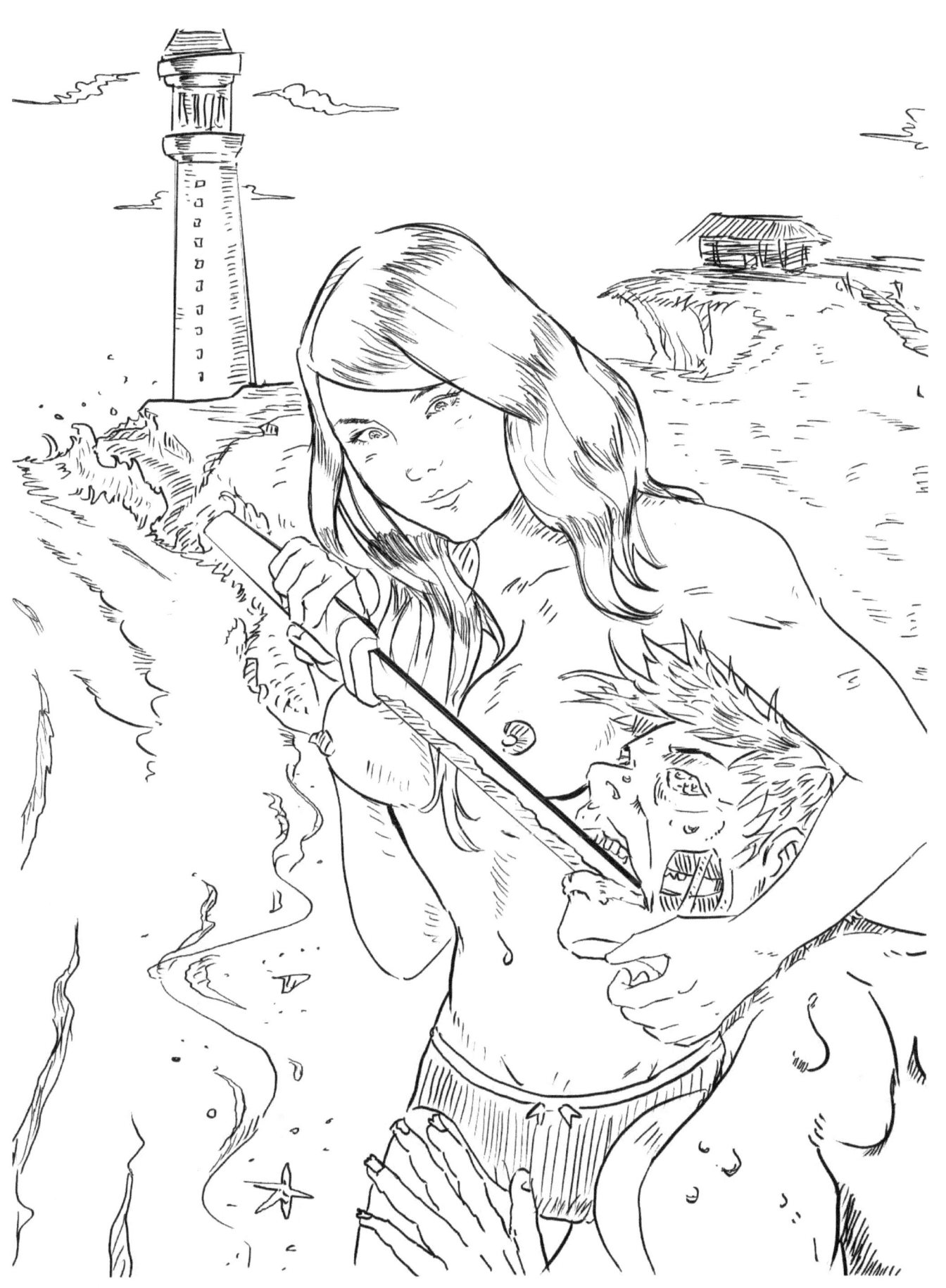

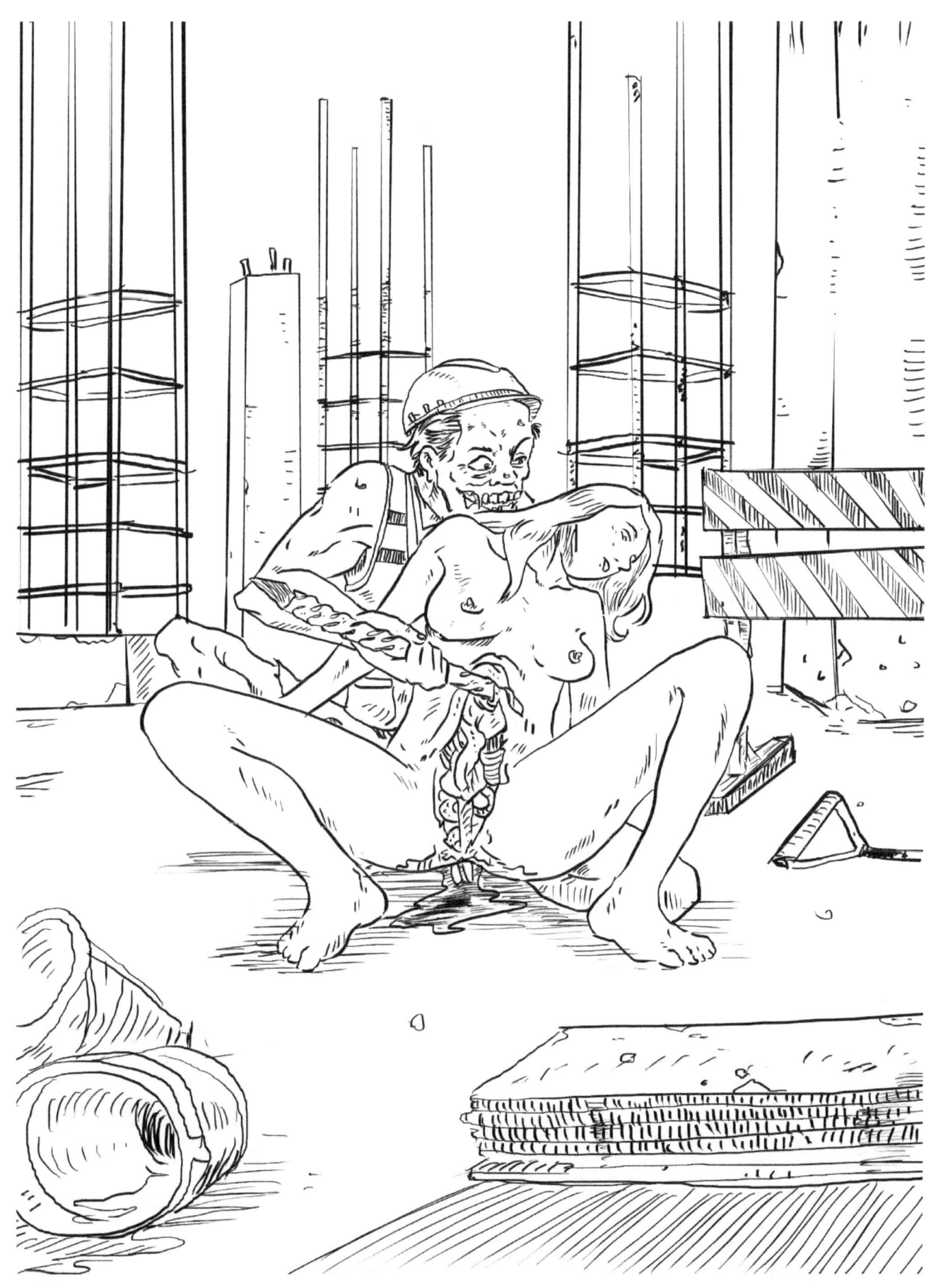

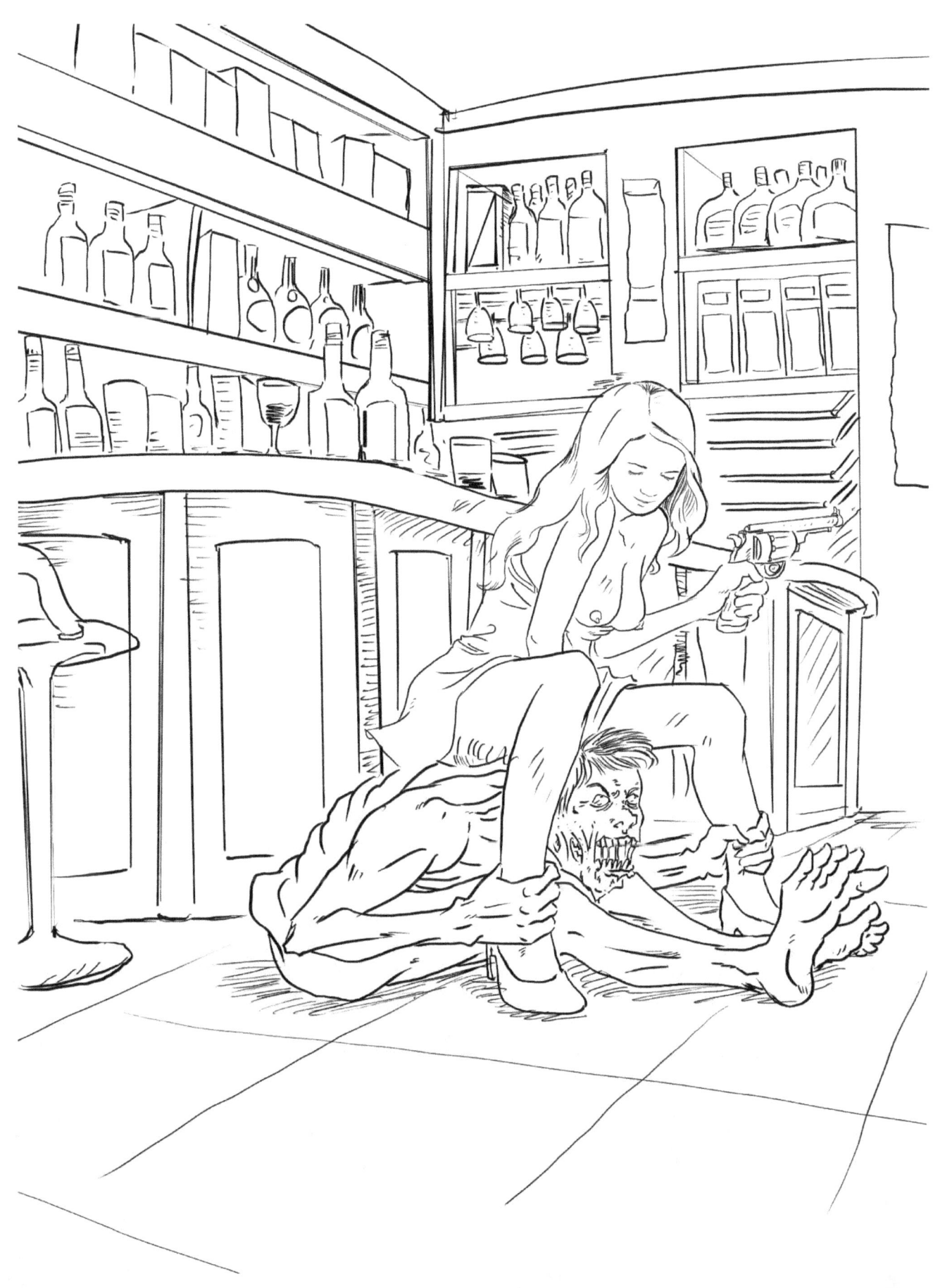

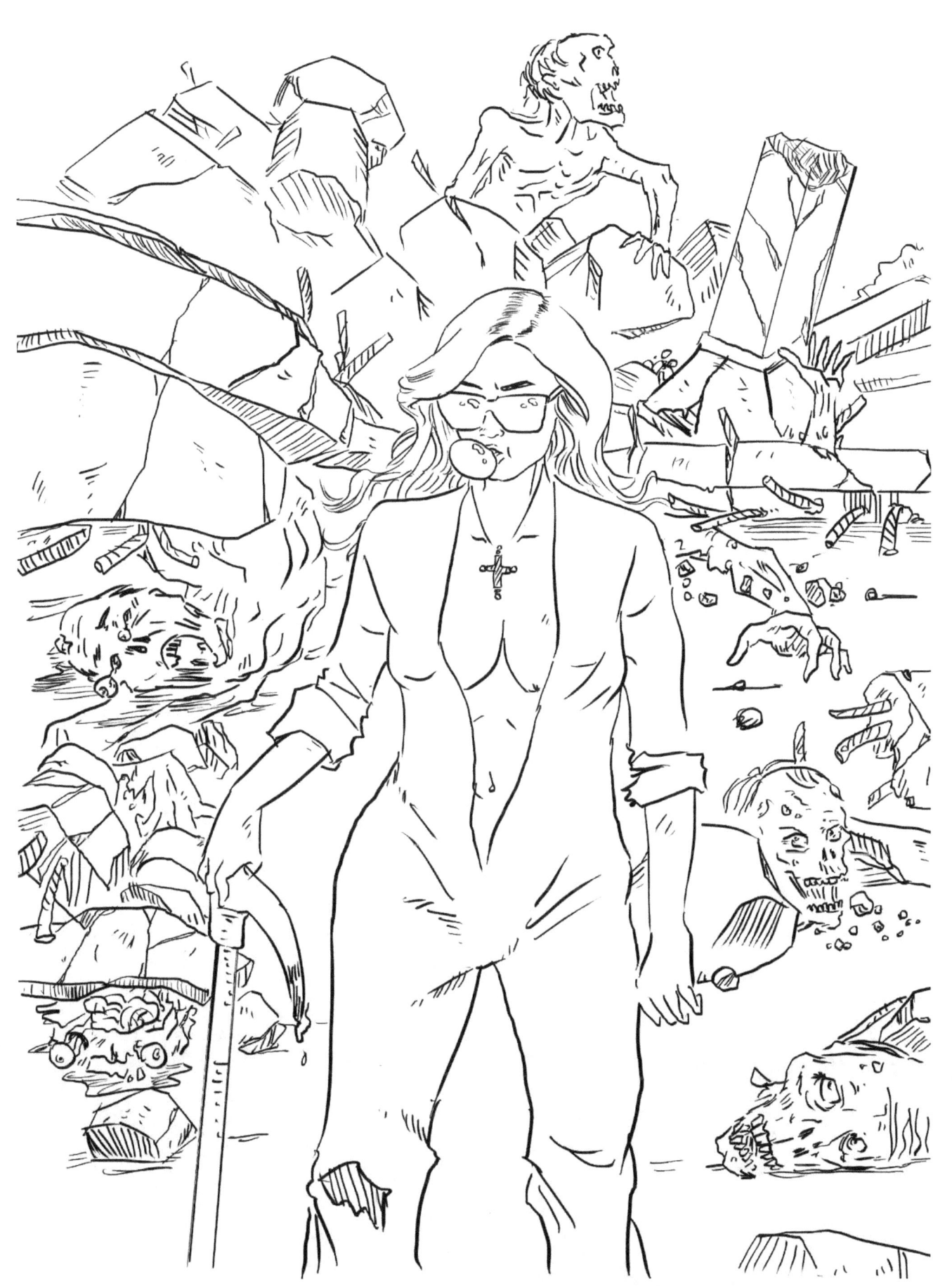

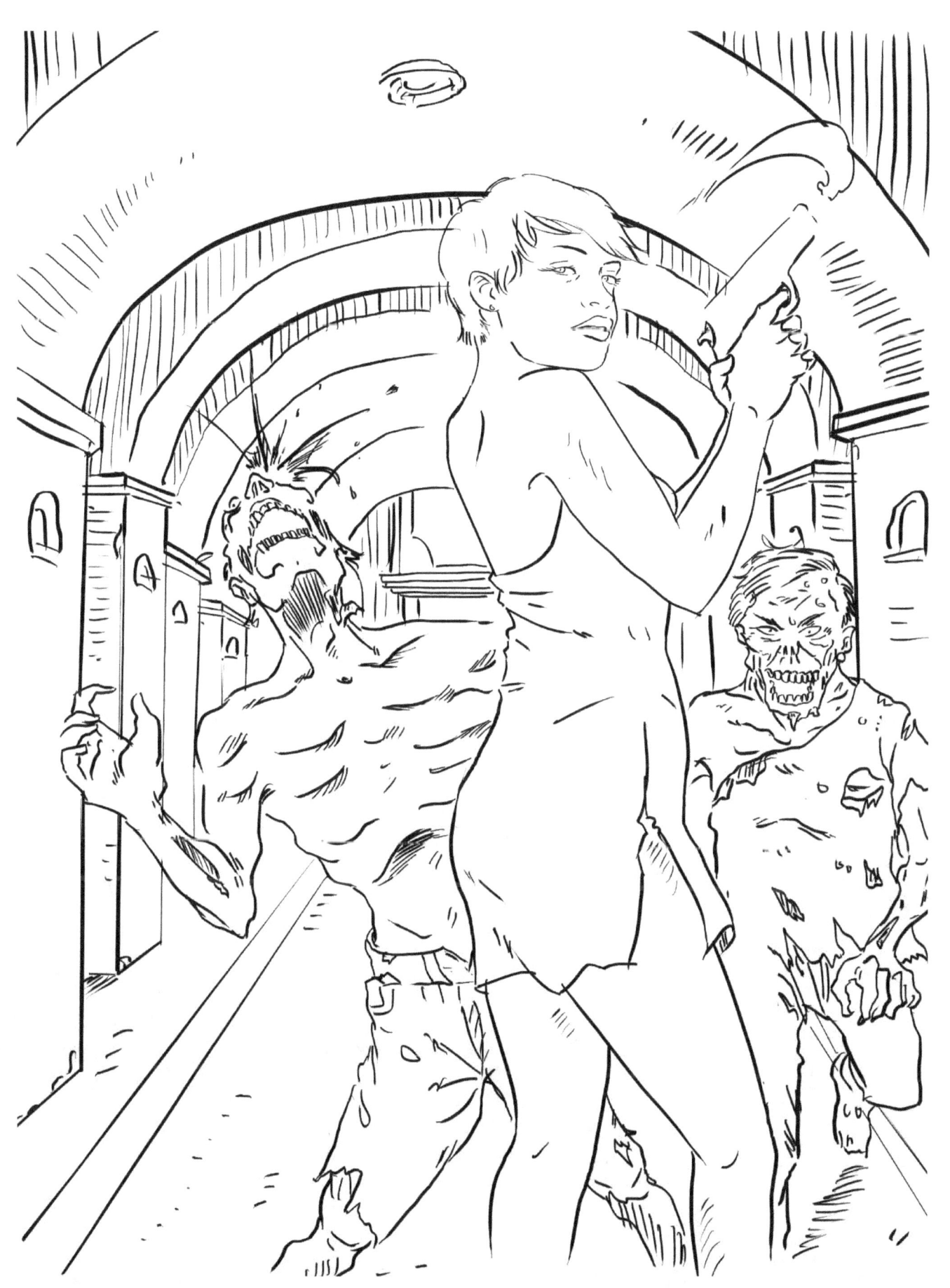

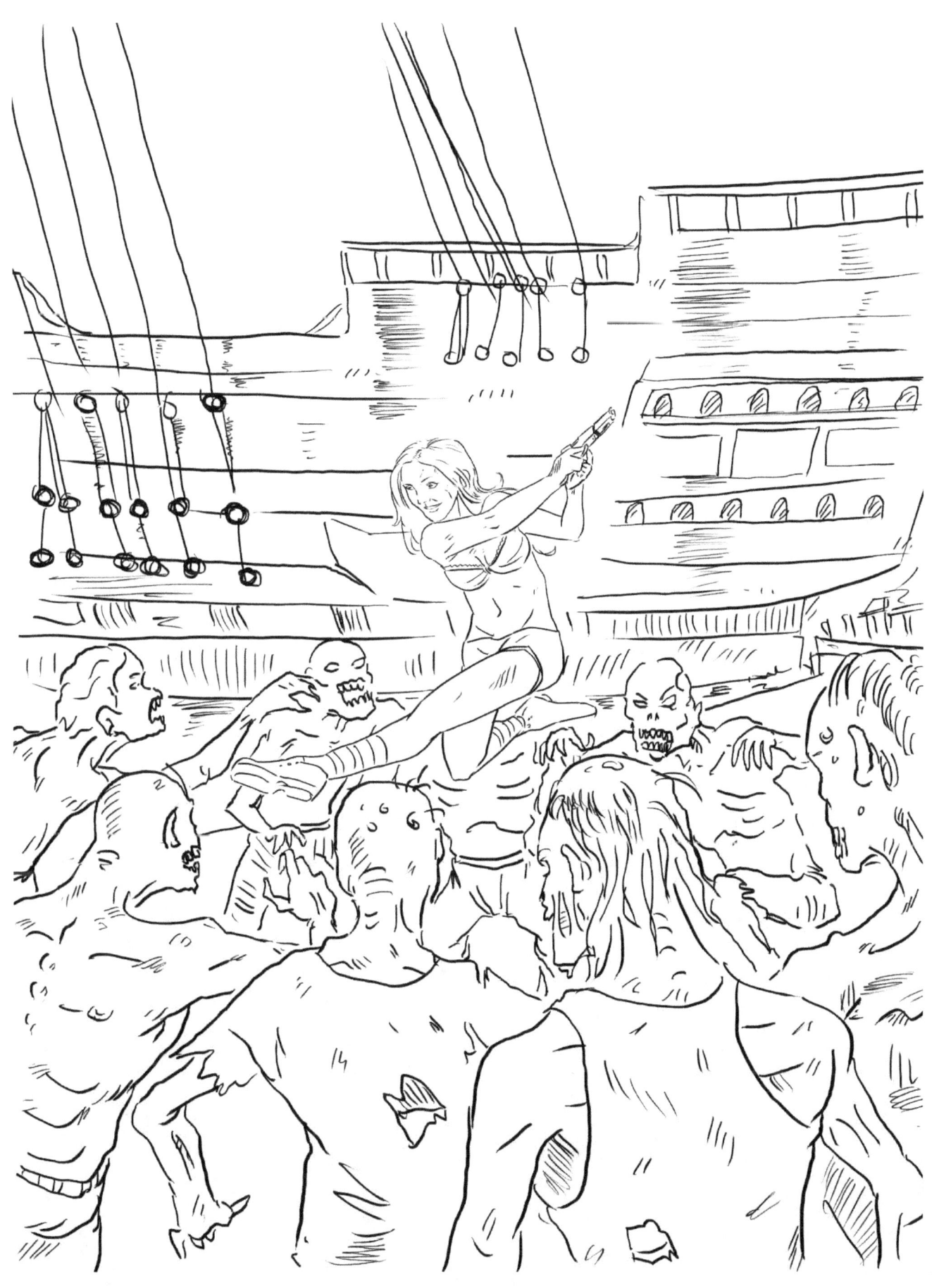

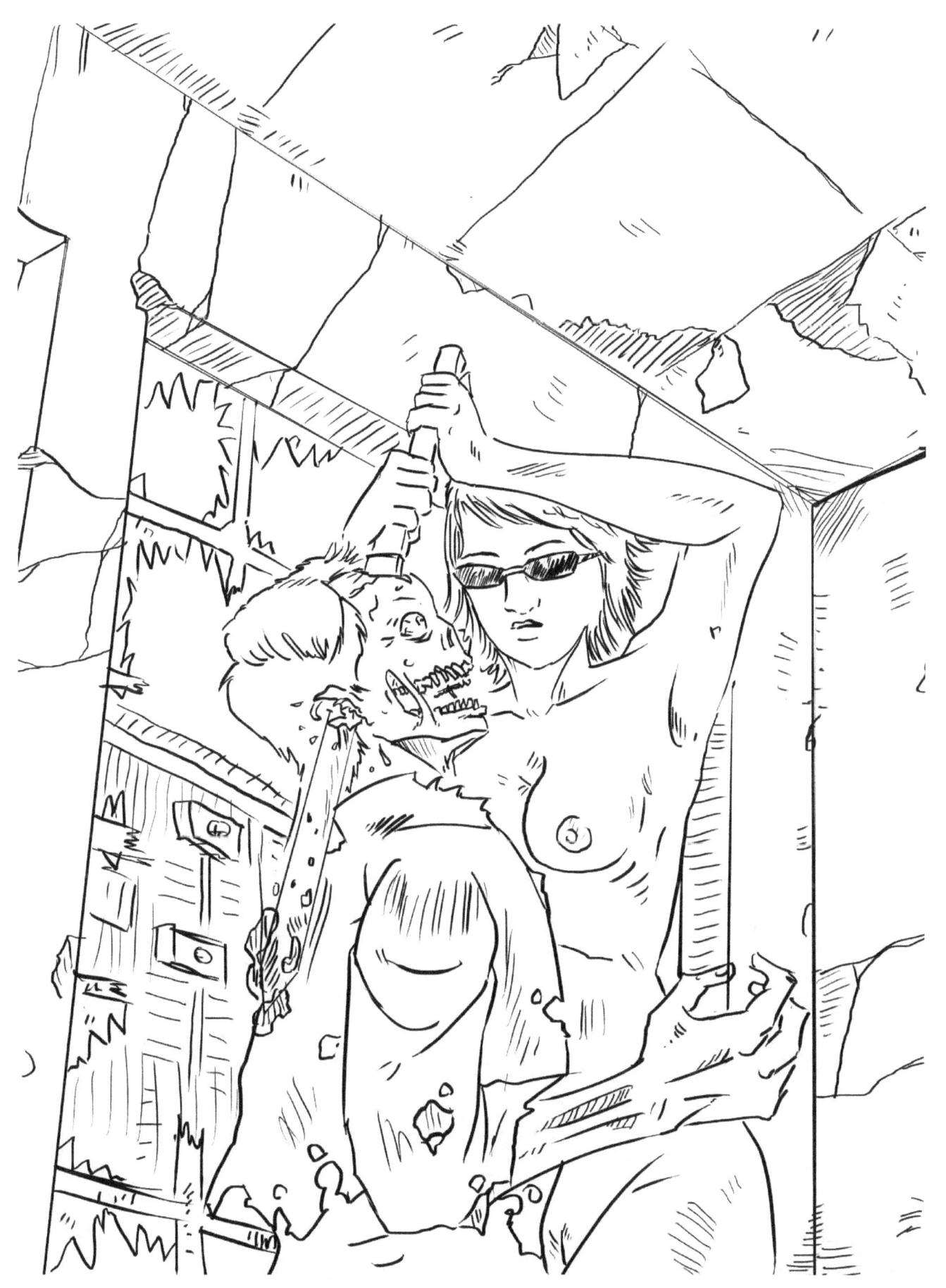

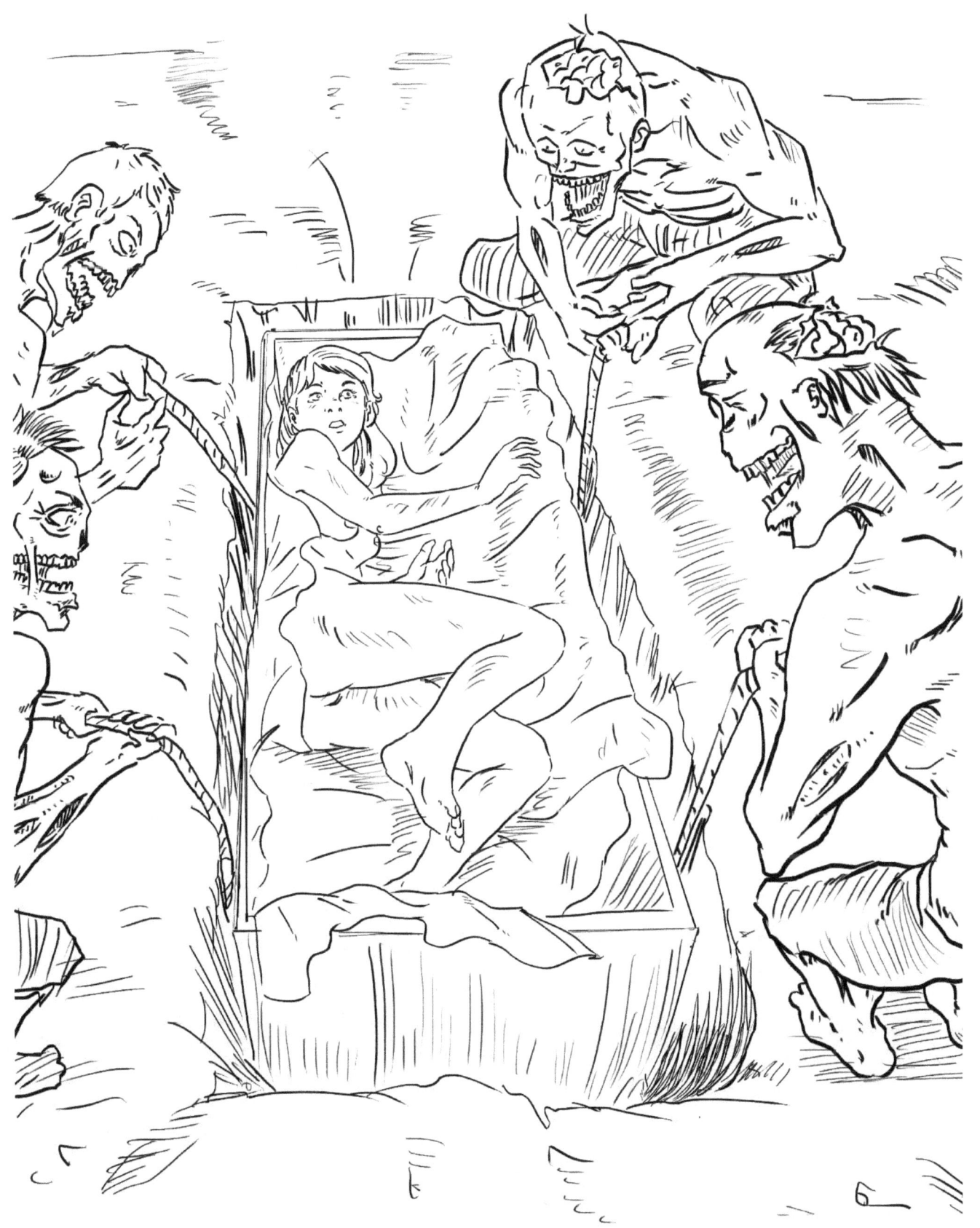

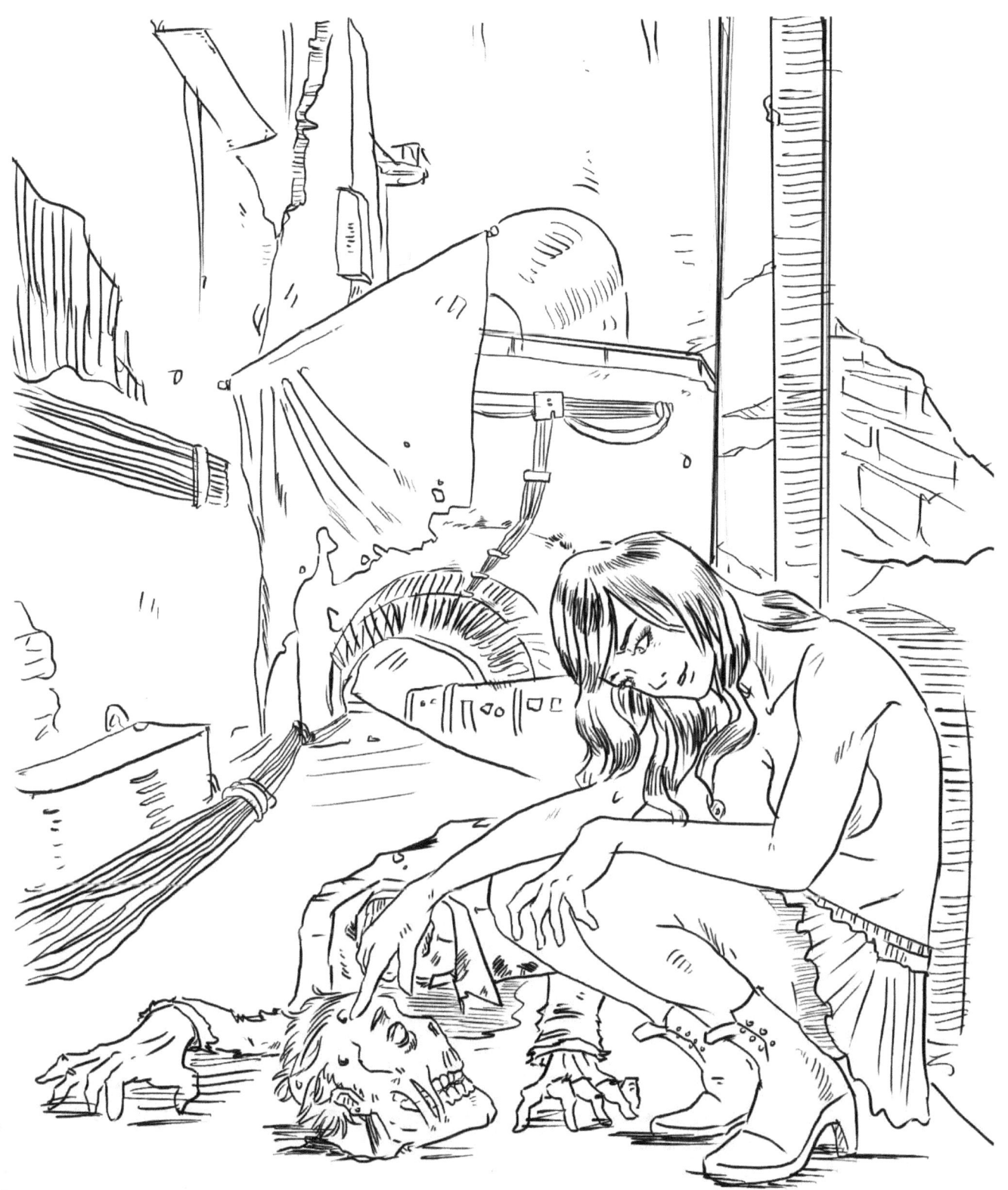

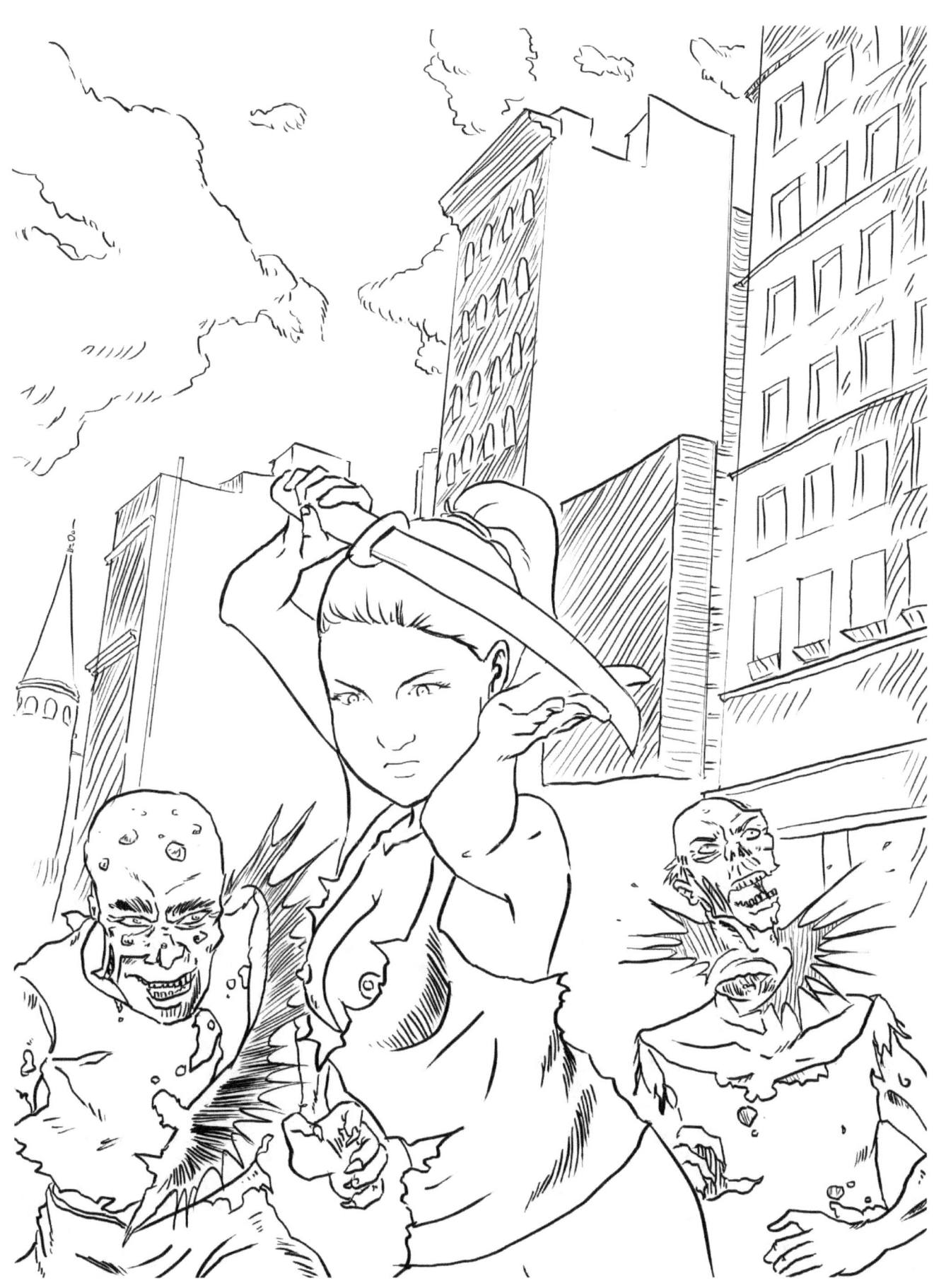

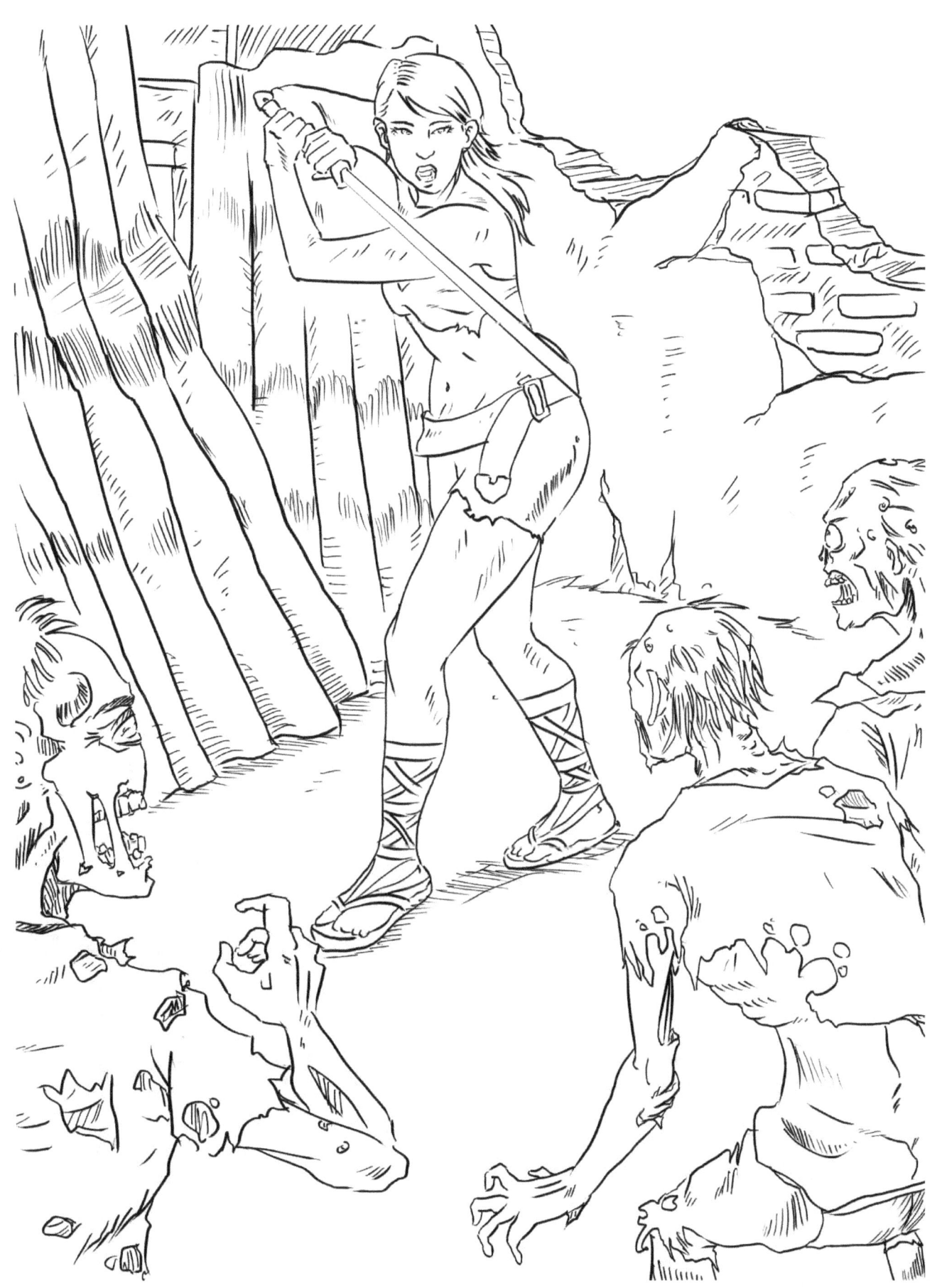

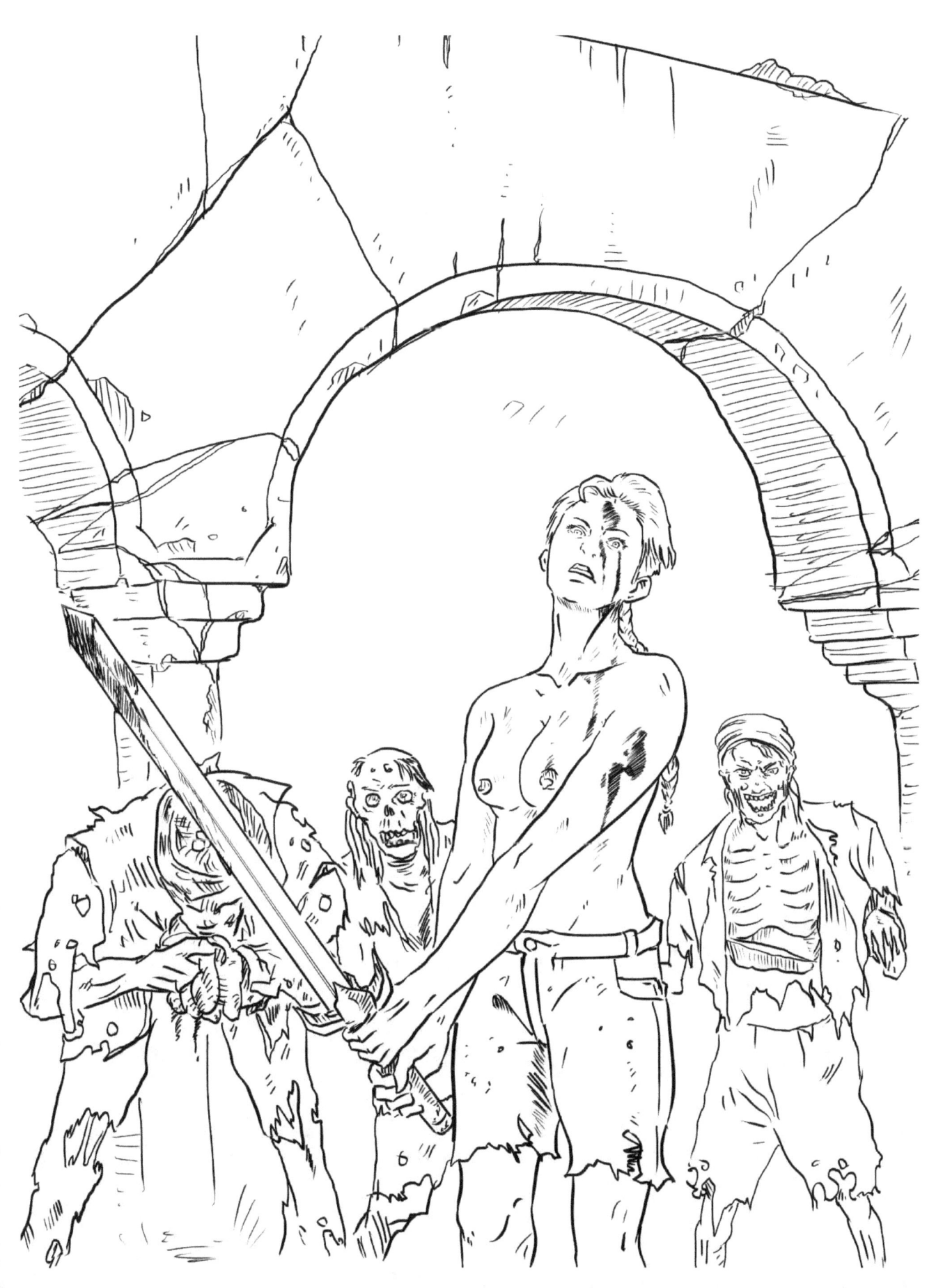

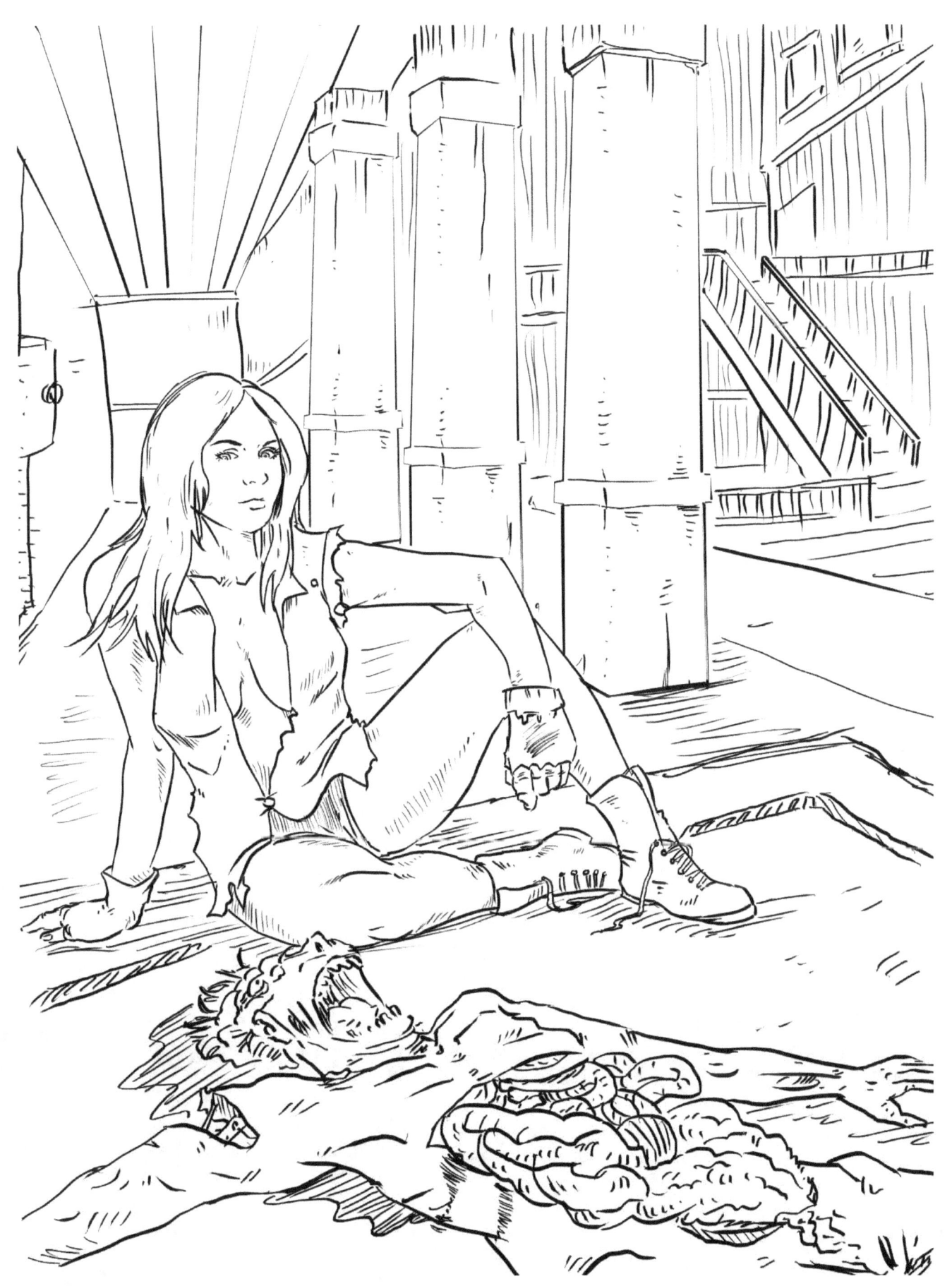

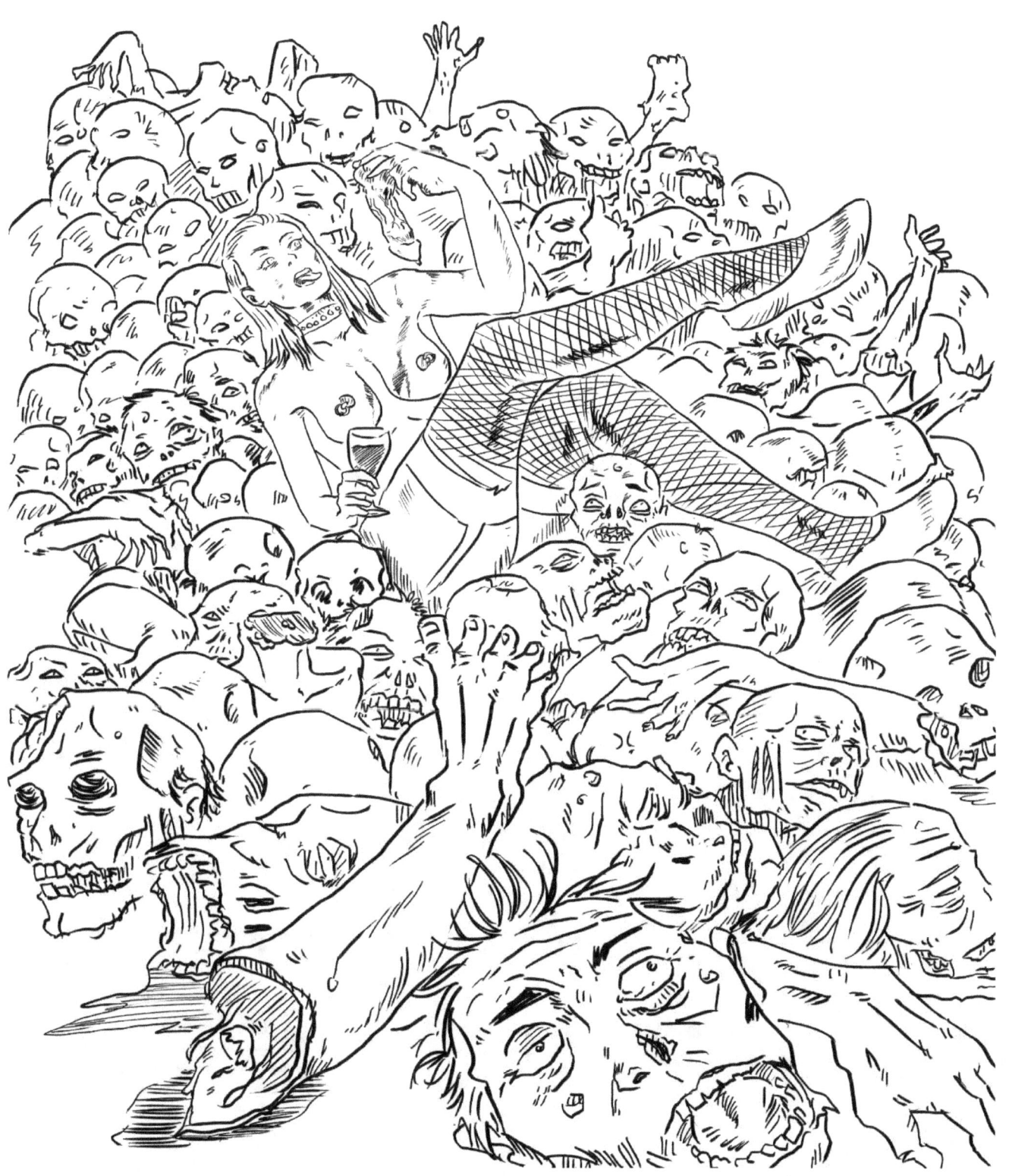

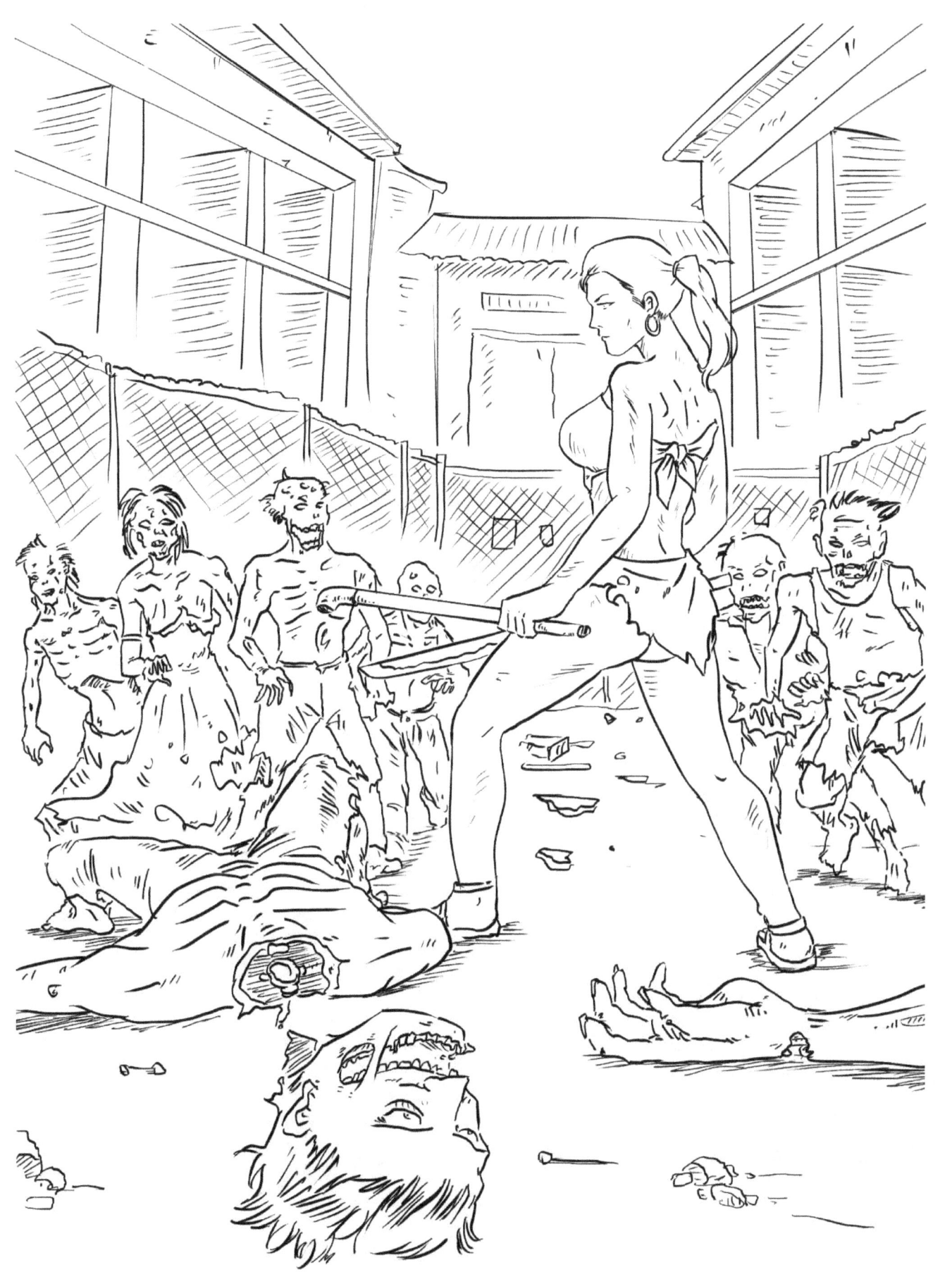

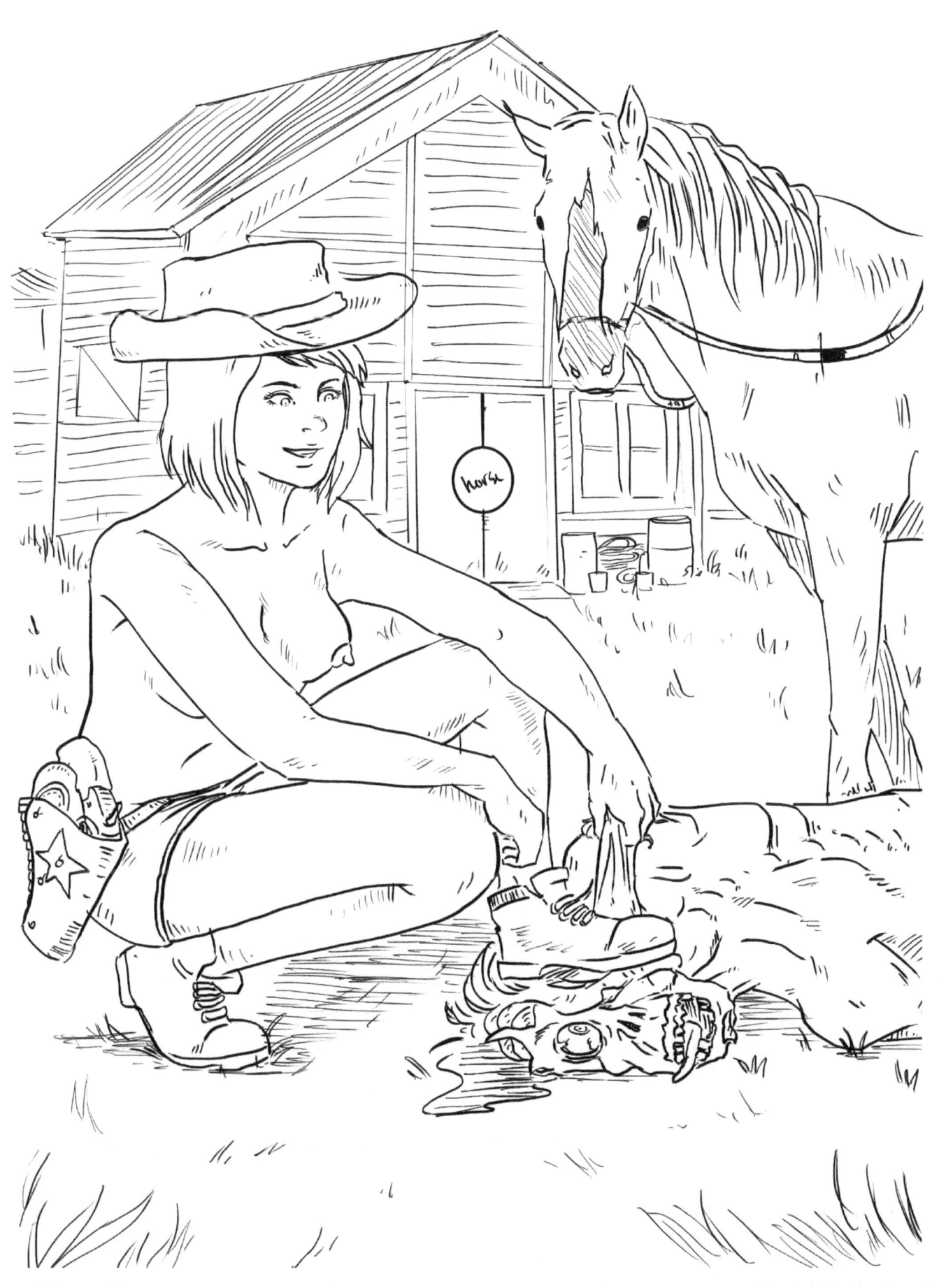

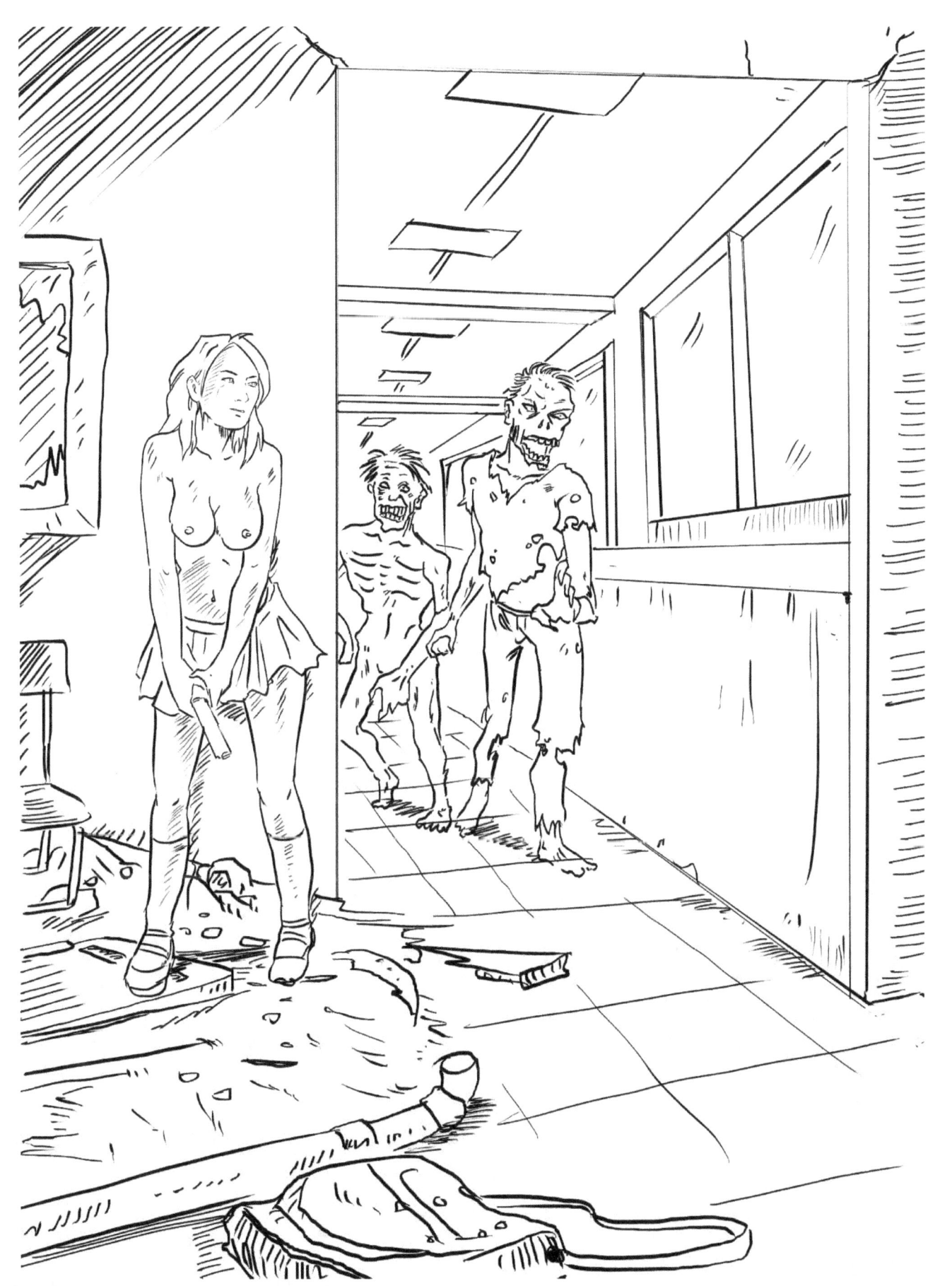

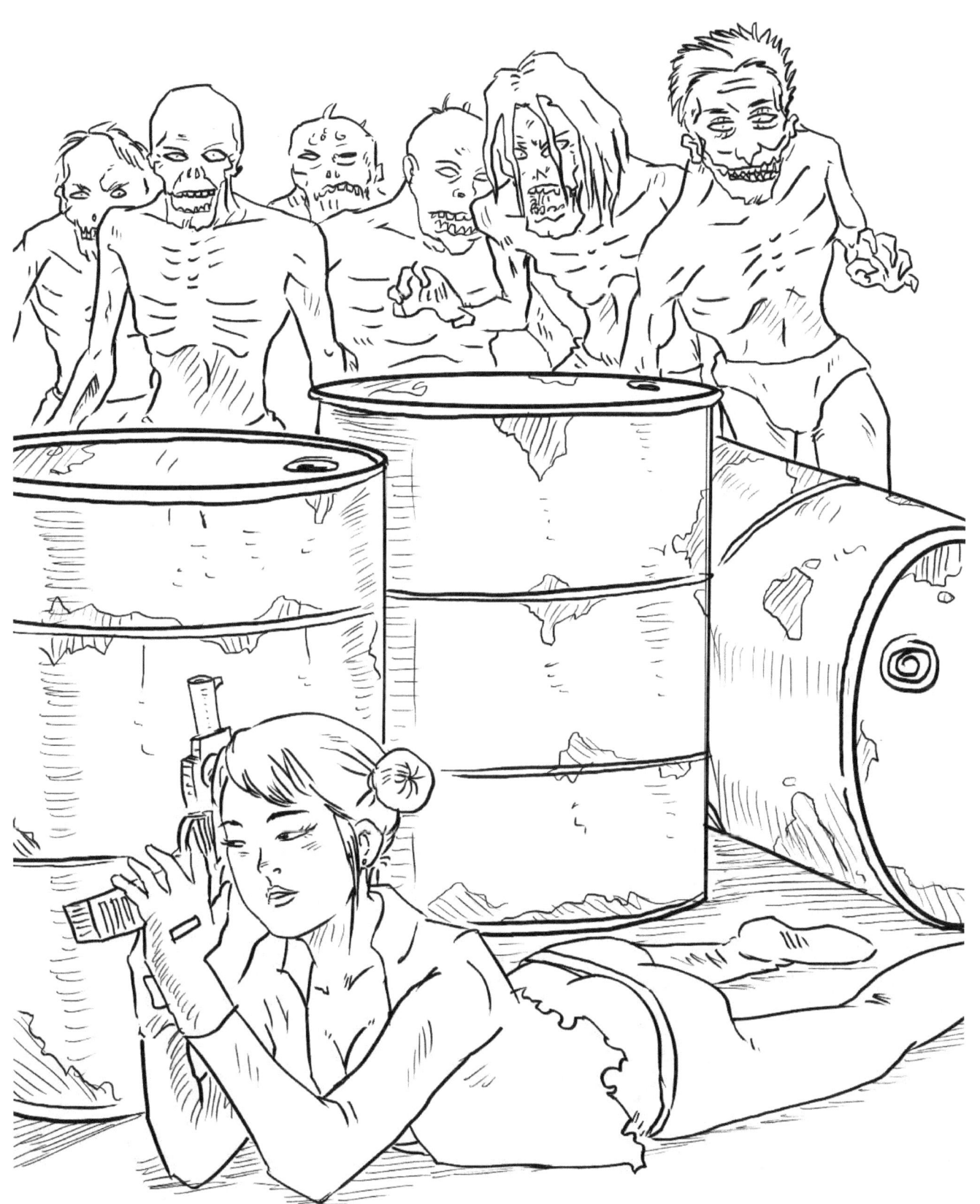

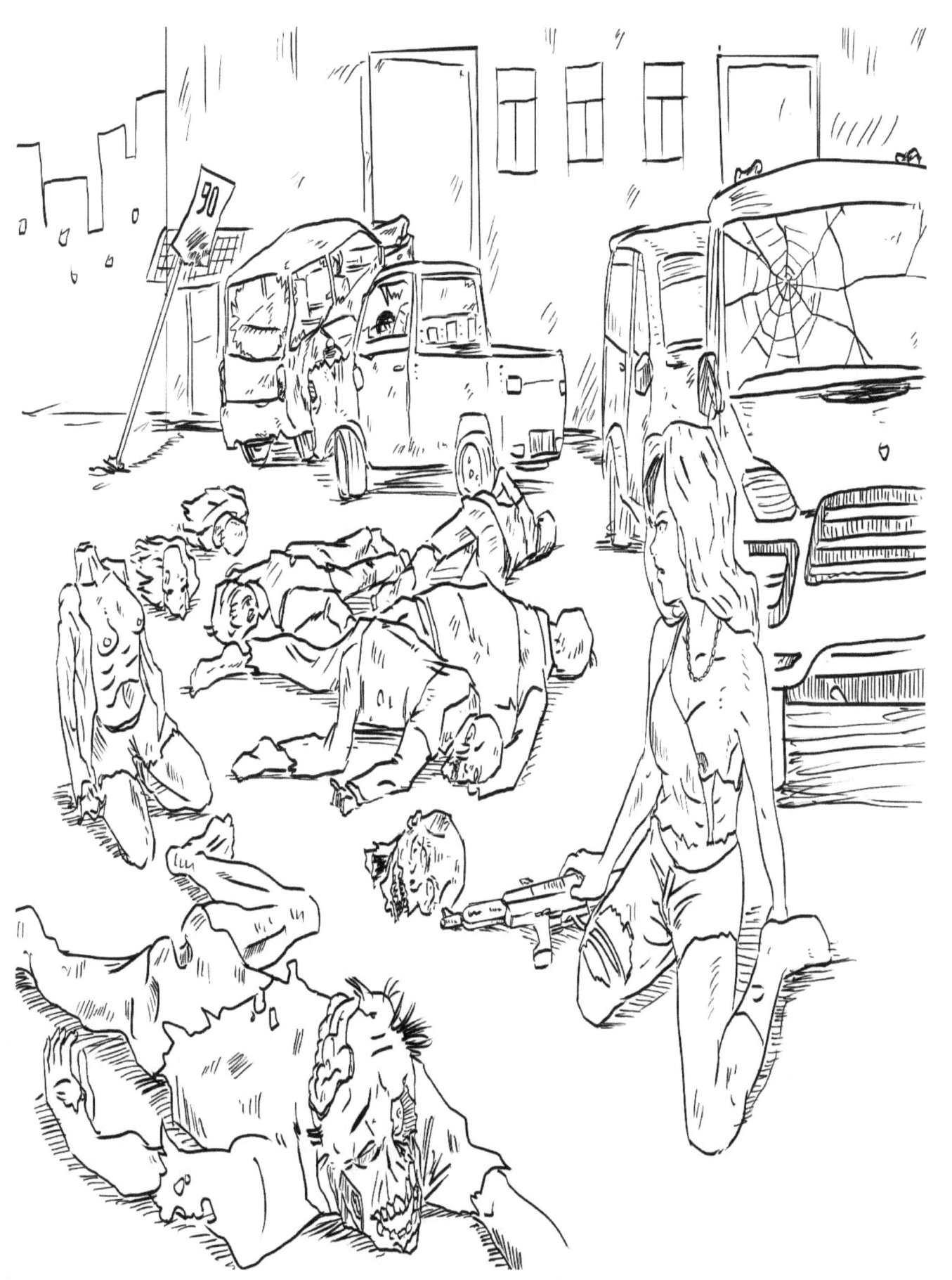

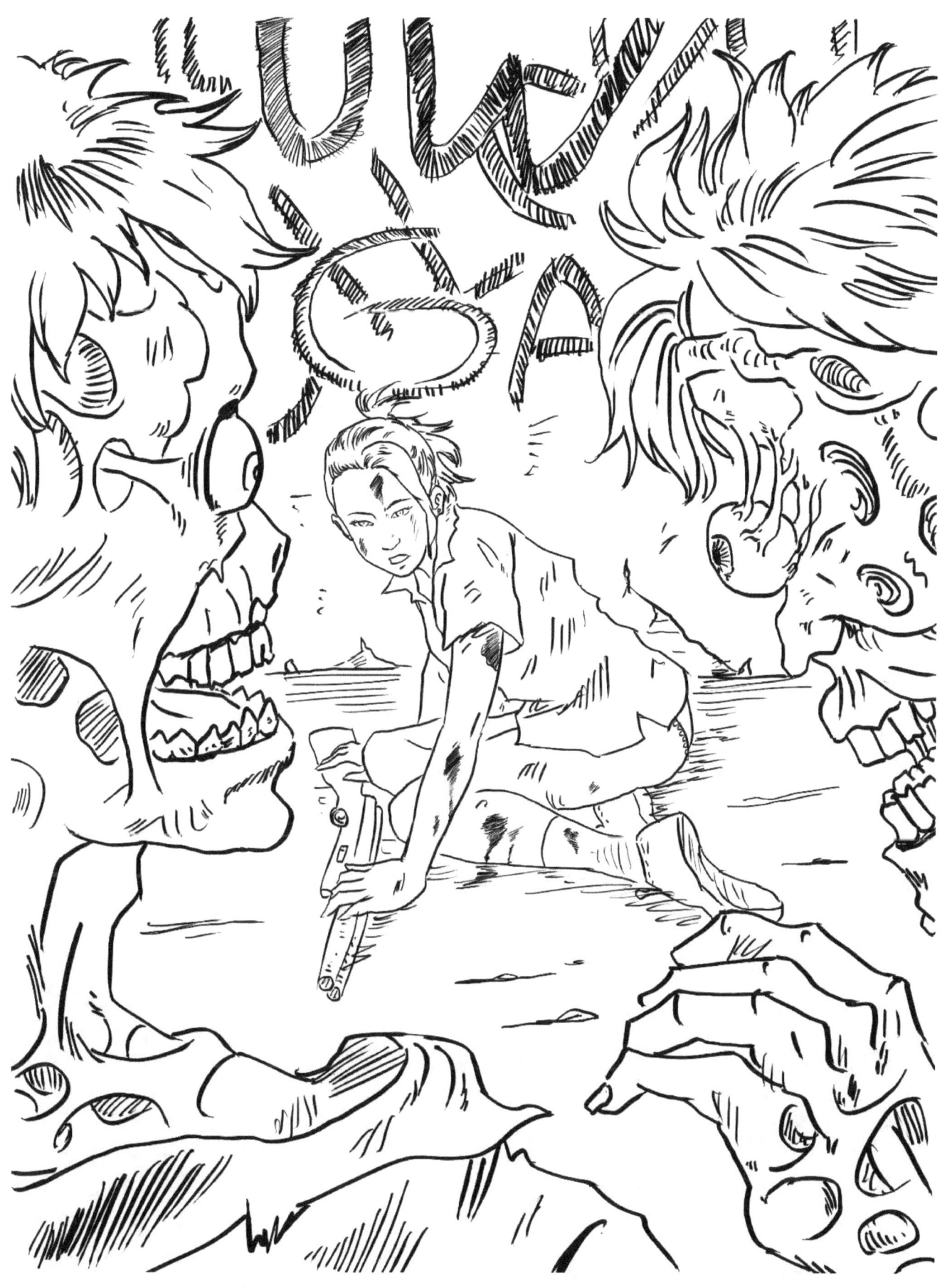

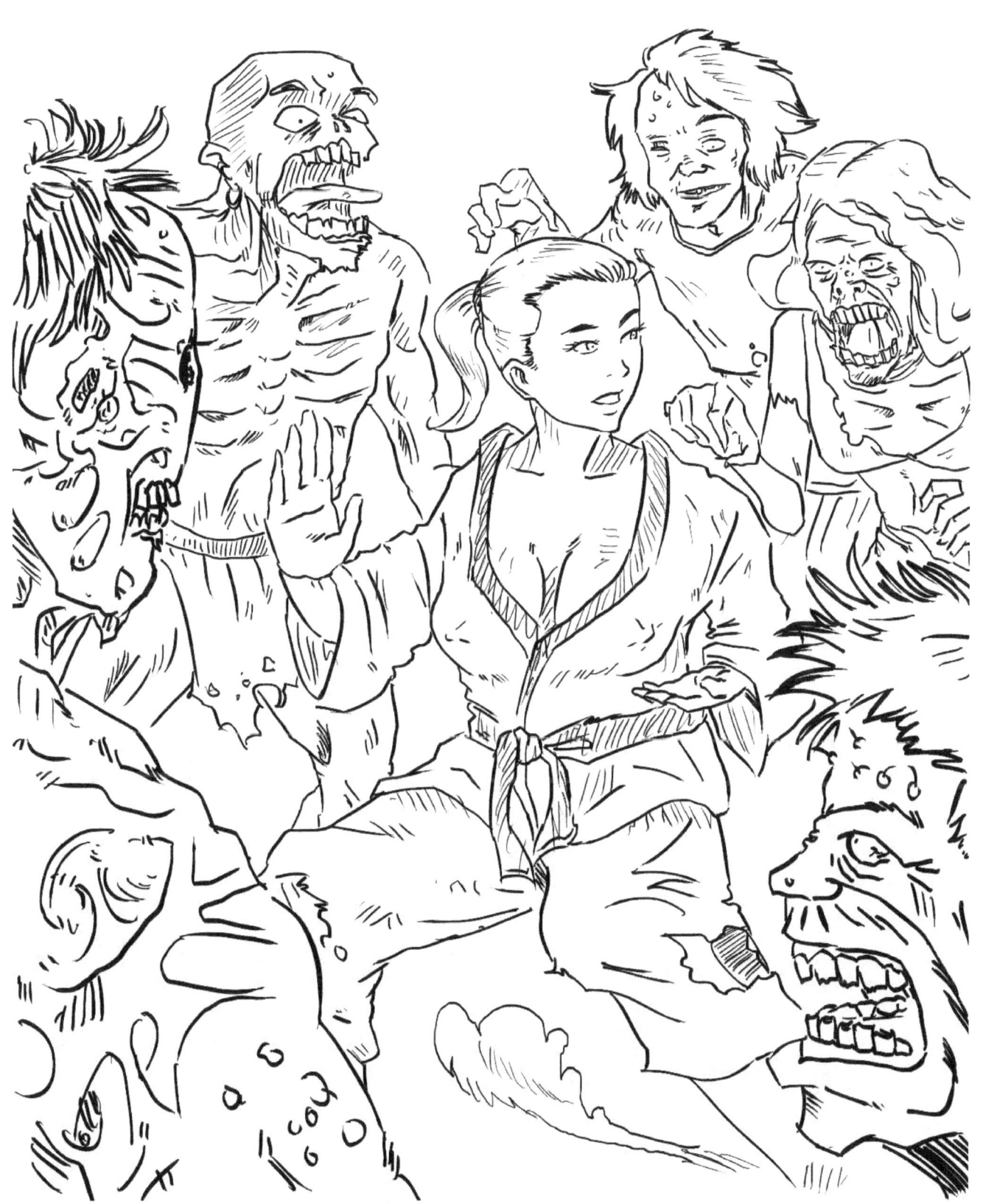

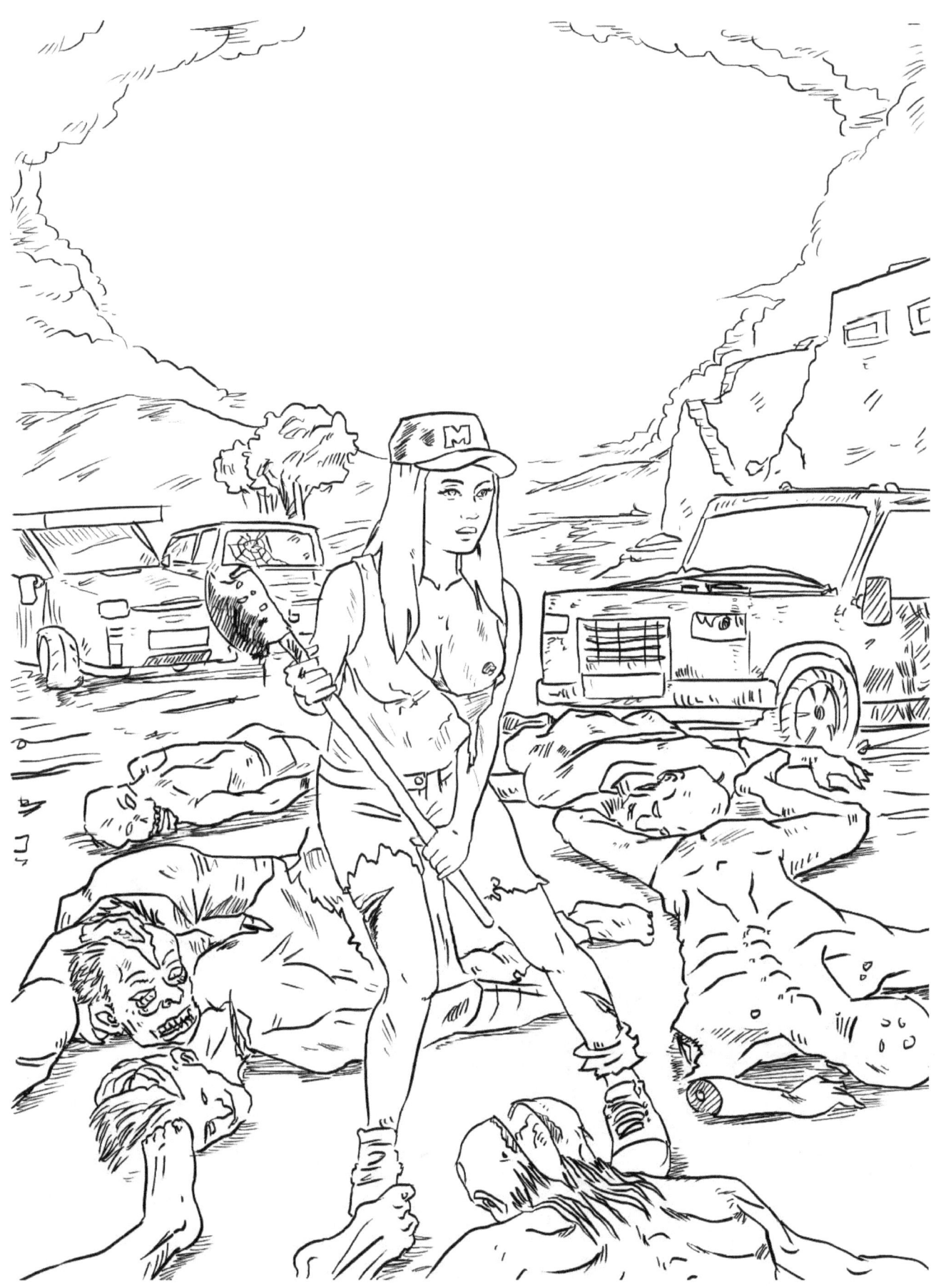

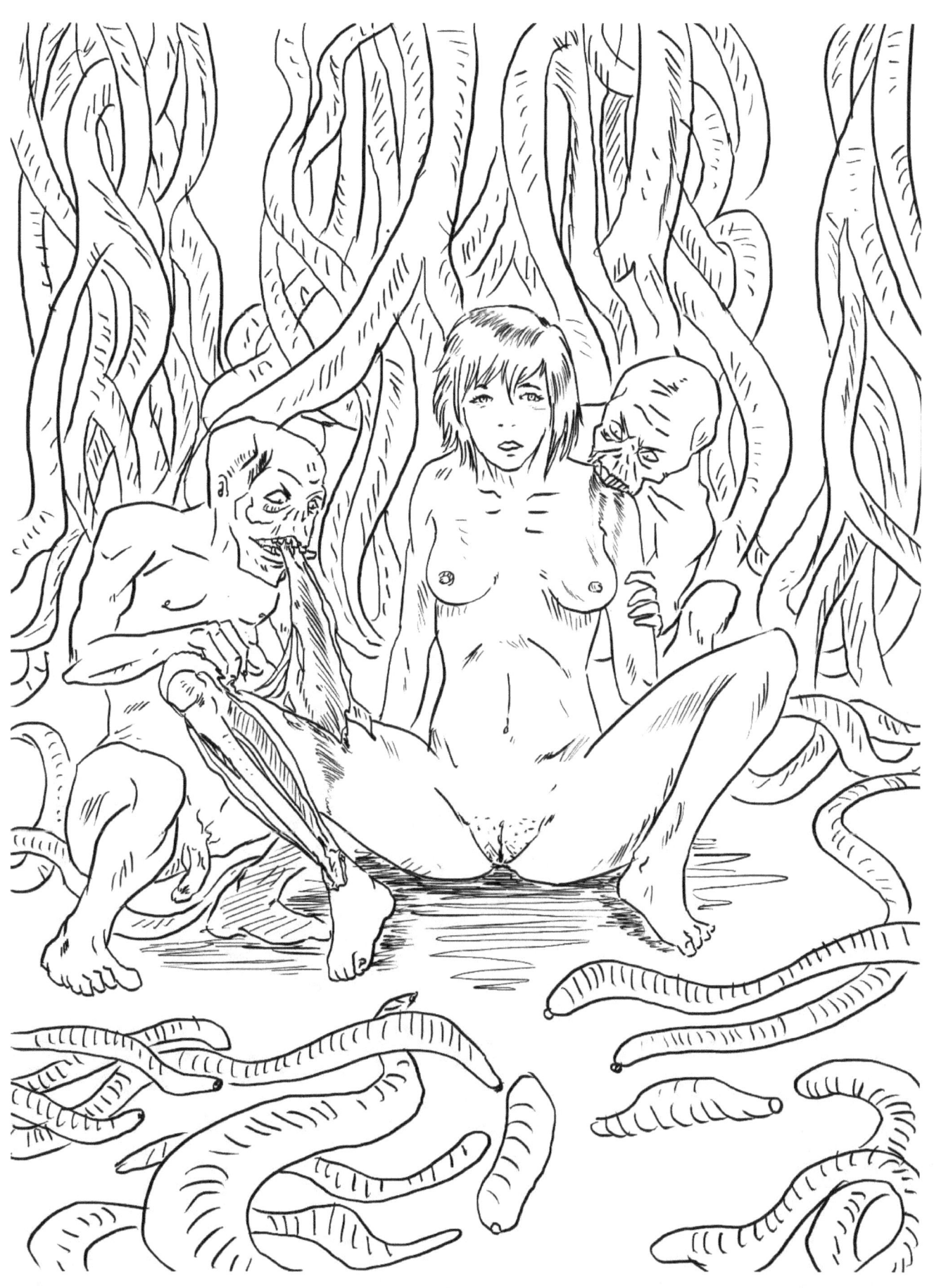

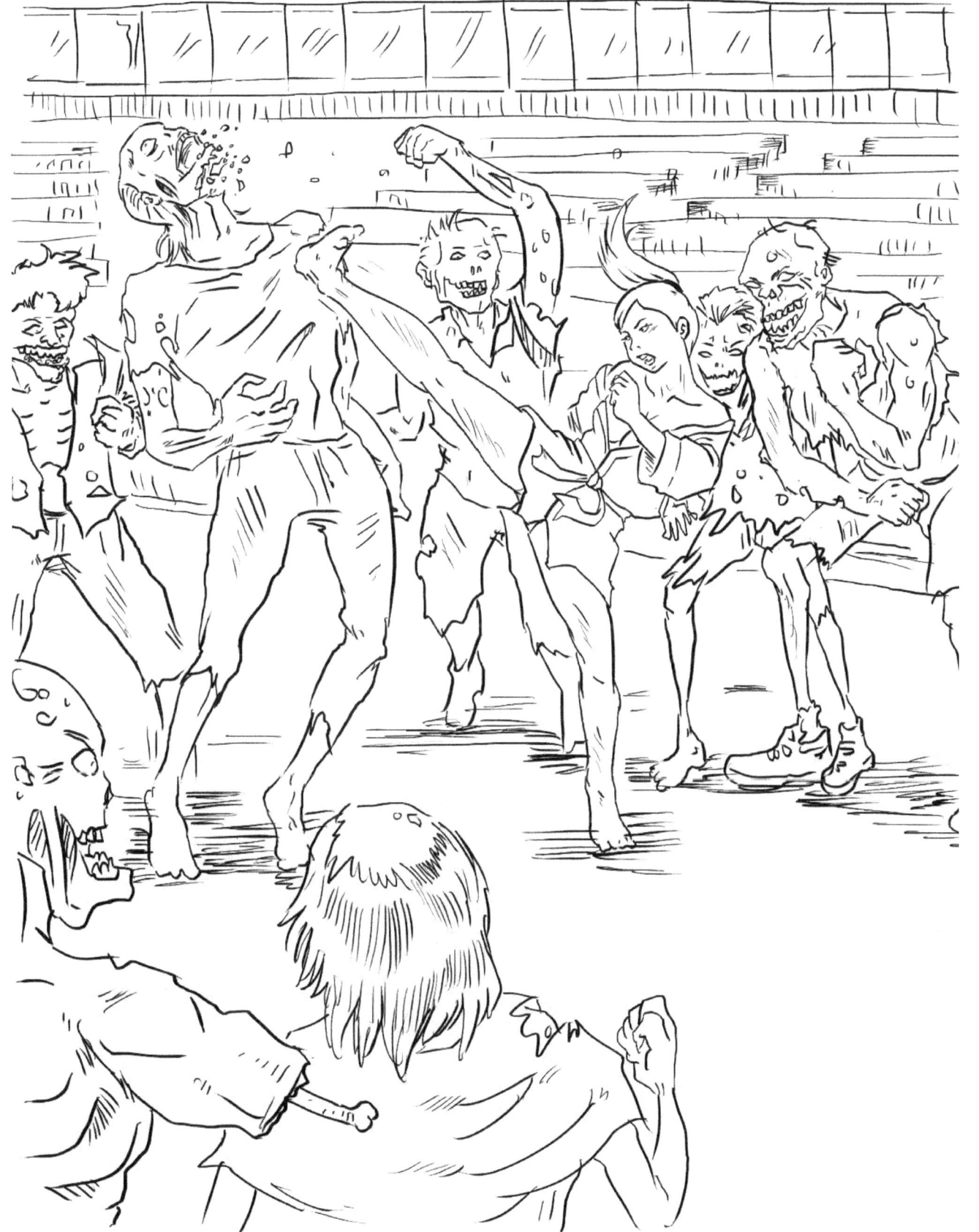

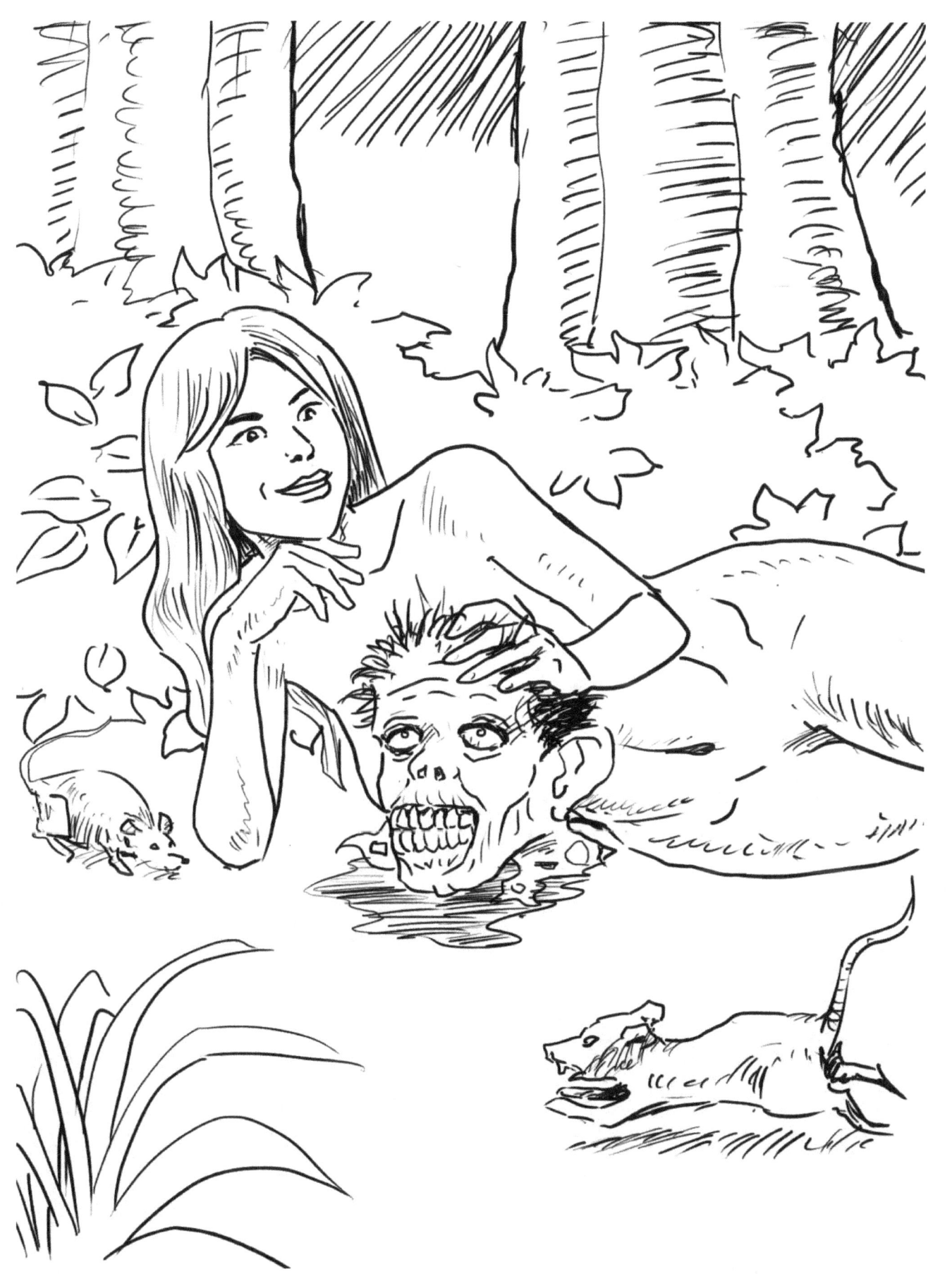

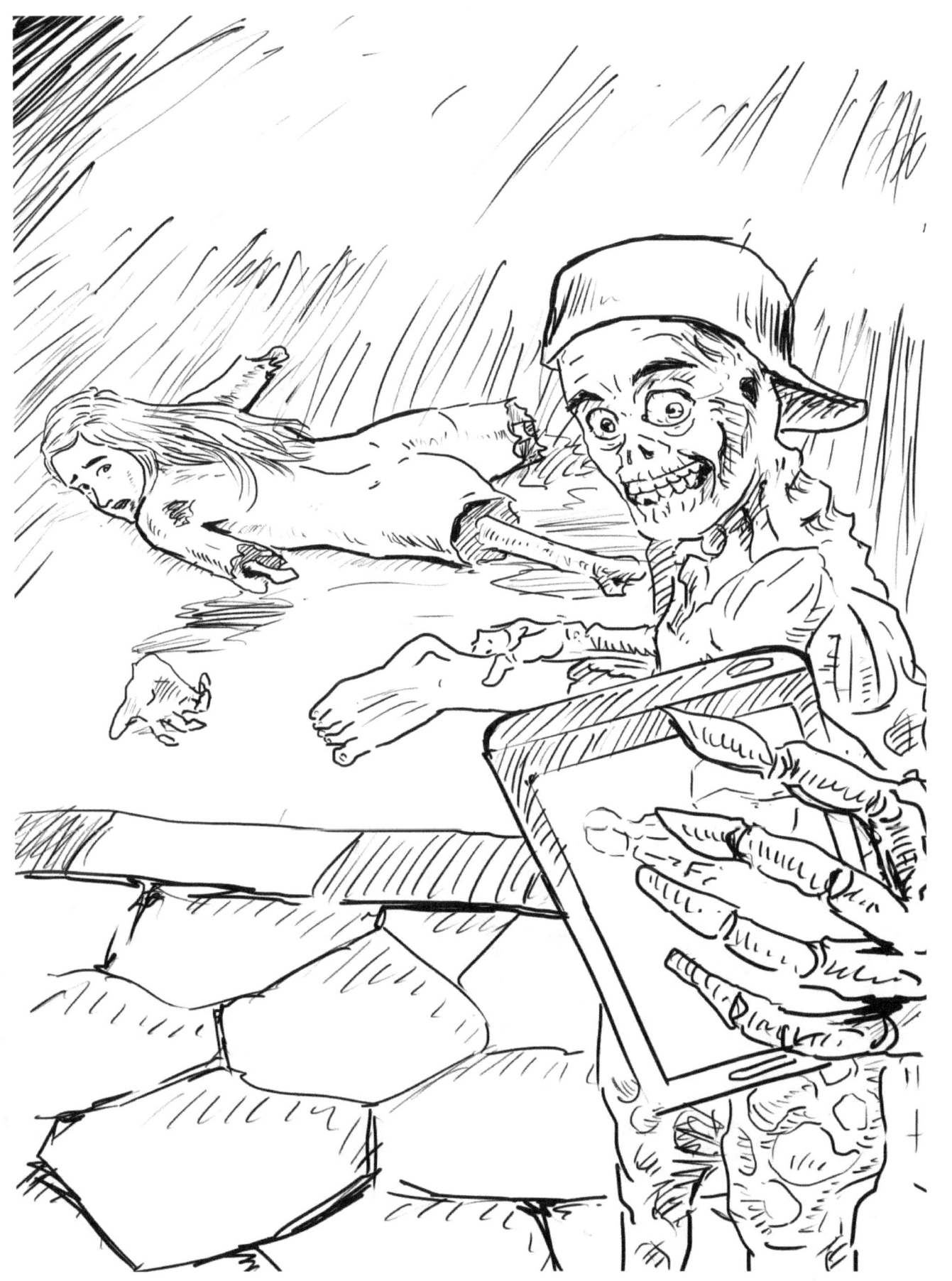

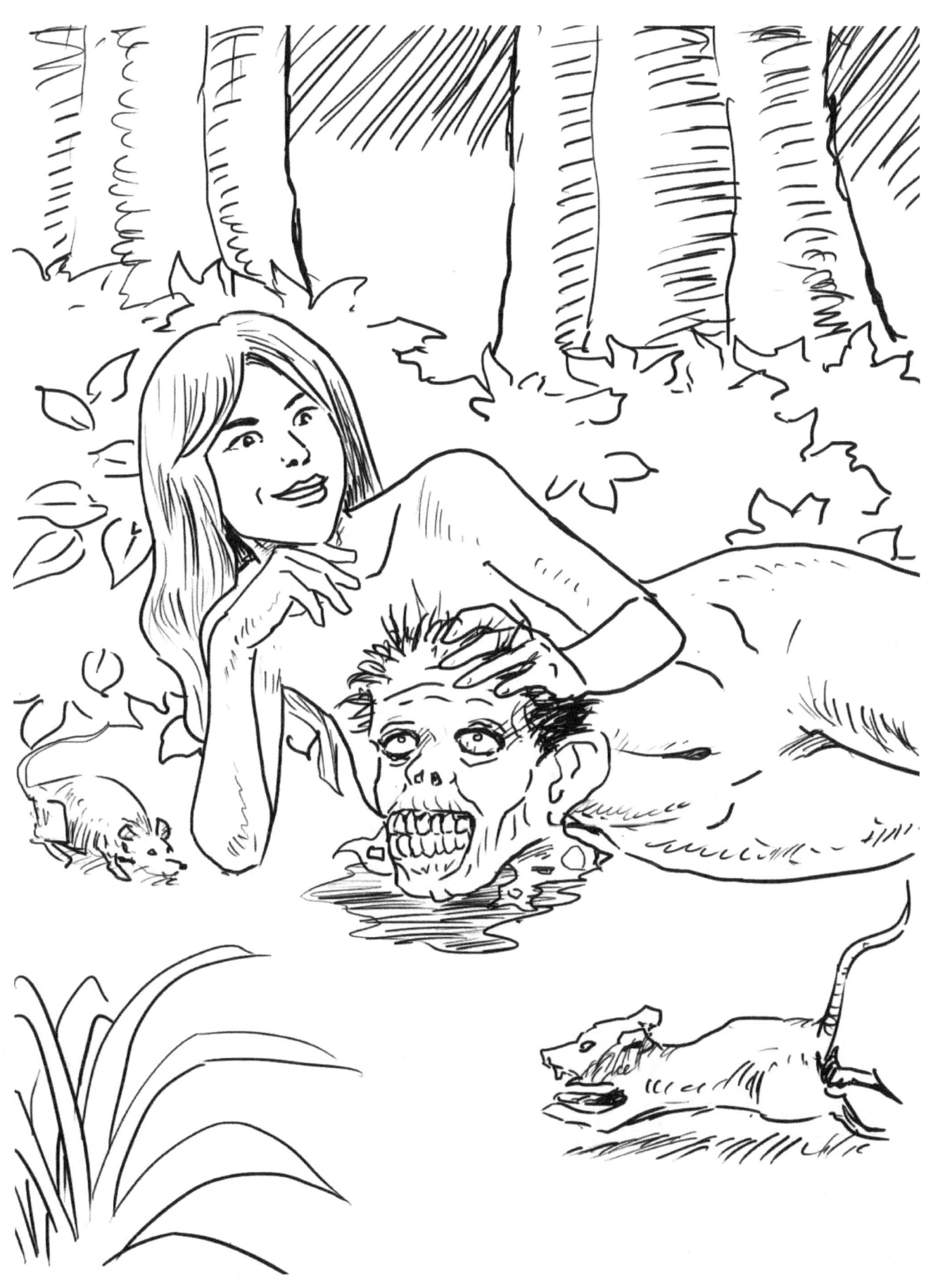

www.ingramcontent.com/pod-product-compliance
Lightning Source LLC
Chambersburg PA
CBHW082338220526
45470CB00008B/2559